*Focus on Hinduism
and Buddhism*

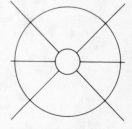

*Robert A. McDermott
Series Editor*

Sarasvatī, as the divine personification of all things flowing, is the Hindu goddess of wisdom. This volume, which seeks to identify the fleeting images projected by film and videotape, as well as the sound of chant and religious song on recordings, appropriately invokes her presence in the placement of this line-drawing as frontispiece. It is our hope that materials cited in the pages that follow may benefit those seeking to learn more about the nature of Hinduism in their on-going study.

Drawing by K. S. Ramu, Madras

FOCUS ON HINDUISM

A Guide to Audio-Visual Resources For Teaching Religion

David J. Dell
David M. Knipe
Robert A. McDermott
Kenneth W. Morgan
H. Daniel Smith

SECOND, ENLARGED EDITION

Revised by H. Daniel Smith
Edited by Robert A. McDermott
With David J. Dell

ANIMA BOOKS, 1981

Focus on Hinduism.

Bibliography: p.
Includes indexes.
1. Hinduism—Study and teaching—Audio-visual aids—Catalogs.
I. McDermott, Robert A.
BL1149.F63   1981   016.2945   81-8085
ISBN 0-89012-018-8   AACR2
ISBN 0-89012-019-6 (pbk.)

This volume is part of a series of guides to the audio-visual materials useful for the study of Hinduism and Buddhism. Preparation and publication of these volumes were made possible by a grant from the National Endowment for the Humanities to the Council on International and Public Affairs, Inc. (Ward Morehouse, President), with Robert A. McDermott, Project Director. Through the Endowment's provision for matching funds, this project was also supported by the Ada Howe Kent Foundation and Baruch College, CUNY.

The first edition of this volume was published as Foreign Area Materials Center Occasional Publication No. 23 (New York: Foreign Area Materials Center, State Education Department, University of the State of New York, and the Council for Intercultural Studies and Programs, 1977). Preparation and publication of this first edition was supported by a grant from the National Endowment for the Humanities to the University of the State of New York, acting as agent for the Council for Intercultural Studies and Programs (Ward Morehouse, President). This project was further assisted by the Ada Howe Kent Foundation, the NDEA Center for South Asian Studies at Columbia University, the Standing Committee on the Study of World Philosophies and Religions (Robert A. McDermott, Chairman) of the Council for Intercultural Studies and Programs.

Printed in USA.

ANIMA BOOKS is a subdivision of Conococheague Associates, Inc., 1053 Wilson Avenue, Chambersburg, Pennsylvania 17201.

Contents

Foreword

THIS REVISED critical guide to the audio-visual materials useful for the study of Hinduism is intended for professors, college students, and independent learners. Along with its companion volume, *Focus on Buddhism*, it has been generously supported by the National Endowment for the Humanities, as well as by several other institutions committed to the task of making audio-visual materials more accessible and intelligible to a wider audience.

The history of this publication, and the project of which it is a part, may be worthy of a brief explanation. Its genesis is traceable to the Project to Strengthen Undergraduate Teaching in Asian Philosophies and Religions (1971–77), made possible by a grant from the National Endowment for the Humanities, the result of which is a seven-volume annotated bibliography for Asian Philosophies and Religions (publication by G. K. Hall, 1979–). At the conclusion of this project, some of the same individuals who had conceived and edited the bibliographies determined to perform a similar service for audio-visual materials. Thanks to the initiative of Ward Morehouse, President of the Council for International and Public Affairs, Inc., a grant application was sent to NEH and a committee was formed consisting of: David J. Dell (Columbia University), David M. Knipe (University of Wisconsin-Madison), Robert A. McDermott (Baruch College, CUNY), Kenneth W. Morgan (Colgate University, Emeritus), and H. Daniel Smith (Syracuse University). This committee produced the first edition of *Focus on Hinduism*, published by the Foreign Area Materials Center and distributed by Learning Resources in International Studies, 1977.

This first edition is indebted to Frederick Blackwell for considerable help with the section on "Hinduism in the West," and to the audio-visual center of his home institution, Washington State University; to Mary Frances Dunham for her research and suggestions concerning reviews of recordings; to Gary Michael Tartakov for finding, viewing, and reporting on slide sets; to the Columbia University South Asia Center for use of its audio-visual facilities and library; and to the producers and distributors who generously loaned their films, videotapes and slides for review.

In both editions Dr. David J. Dell coordinated the review of slide sets and recordings and was primarily responsible for the compilation of the various appendices.

Upon publication of the 1977 edition of *Focus on Hinduism*, an ambitious project was conceived for a comprehensive review of audio-visual materials on Buddhism, as well as for a series of essay-guides primarily for use in college courses on Hinduism and Buddhism. In order for these thematic guides (see back cover) to make fullest possible use of both "Focus" guides, the committee determined to revise and update *Focus on Hinduism* and publish it as a companion to *Focus on Buddhism*. For this demanding task, the committee turned to its member who had been at the forefront of this field for many years, Professor H. Daniel Smith. Anyone who has worked with Professor Smith, or has seen any of his eleven films on Hinduism (*Image India*), must be aware of the fine blend of expertise and diligence which he brings to his work. Happily for all of us who will be using this guide in years to come, Professor Smith brought these same qualities to the preparation of this edition of *Focus on Hinduism*

Robert A. McDermott

Preface

THE PRESENT edition, revised and enlarged from the version published in 1977, incorporates several changes which distinguish it from the earlier publication. Most noteworthy are the rearrangements of the internal divisions and the inclusion of some recently produced resources resulting in additional reviews. Some sections containing indices and reference materials have also been expanded or added. A number of minor emendations have been made, among them revision upward of the figures quoted for rental and purchase of many items; the cost figures now presented are those which pertain at press time. It may be expected that in reflection of a spiraling inflation, actual charges will continue to rise after the publication of this volume.

In the earlier version, the central portions featured as separate major sections all films and videocassettes reviewed, all slide sets and filmstrips seen, and all recordings audited; those sections were each subdivided, then, according to categories of contents. The present new arrangement brings together all resources, regardless of medium, into one of three pedagogical categories. Thus, all the films, videotapes, slides, filmstrips, microfiche archives, and recordings appropriate for learning about Hinduism as a religious tradition are found in the first section of reviews. All the materials pertinent to the cultural background for the study of Hinduism are clustered in the second section. The samplings of resources that reflect the interplay of Hinduism and the West are reviewed in the third section. Accordingly, the instructor preparing a particular program of pedagogy will now find in once section the full array of available items conveniently grouped. It is hoped that the present arrangement will serve to encourage users to consider, for example, reinforcing the gains of screening a film with the supplementary playing of relevant recordings, and/or the showing of related slides in order to achieve maximum impact on the learning process, a process, the editor suggests, which now more than ever before can appropriately utilize visual images and sound signals alongside the printed book, the conventional lecture presentation, and the informal discussion session.

The assignment to one of the three pedagogical categories of certain films, slides, or recordings is, and remains, controversial. Those who have worked on this project remain sensitive to the issues

involved even as this new edition goes to press. Occasional crosslist-
ings serve to emphasize the multipurpose nature of many instructional materials under review. It should be stressed that the assignment of any particular resource to one of the three categories
carries with it neither automatic commendation nor automatic
condemnation; the categories are nothing more than devices to
identify a resource as most pertinent to a pedagogical context. Within
that pedagogical context, however, a conscientious attempt has been
made by the reviewers to evaluate the learning potential of every film
and slide set, filmstrip, and recording noticed. Hence, each category
contains resources some of which have received laudatory reviews and
some of which have been roundly criticized for shortcomings. To
illustrate: simply because a film is placed in the first category,
HINDUISM AS A RELIGIOUS TRADITION, does not necessarily
mean it is recommended e.g., see review of *The Hindu World* in Part
One.

I am pleased to have been given broad editorial responsibility for
this enlarged and updated version of *Focus on Hinduism*. This task
was made easier by the help of both Dr. David M. Knipe and Dr. David
J. Dell, each of whom served as second evaluator on several new items
included in this volume; their cautions and contributions were most
helpful. A special word of thanks to Professor Robert A. McDermott
who, as overall administrator of a project in which my endeavor was
only a small part, did much to facilitate my efforts. I can only reiterate
the hope expressed three years ago by all those who labored with such
devotion on the first edition, that this effort may prove useful to all for
whom the sights and sounds of Hinduism are crucial data in this
study.

H. Daniel Smith

Syracuse University
August 1979

Introduction

THIS WORK is designed for anyone seeking an understanding of Hinduism who recognizes the need to augment printed resources with visual and audio materials. It is addressed to students, teachers, and interested individuals—to anthropologists, musicologists, sociologists, historians of religion, art, music, dance, literature, and drama, to librarians and museologists, as well as to many outside academia who share the concern for a clearer understanding of Hinduism. It also has in mind a variety of professional audio-visual people, media distributors and producers, film and video makers, and photographers who may find this guide of some use.

It is intended to further our comprehension of a remarkable religion that now, after several generations of Western scholarship, is recognized as a dynamic, complex, and sophisticated aggregate of myths, rites, symbols, and doctrines not readily comprehensible from reading books *about* them.

Unfortunately, because of the nature of our educational experience, if we allow any time at all to the study of religion we spend that time in classrooms reading and talking about religious expressions X or Y or Z. But religious activities, expressions of religious experience, the religious life itself, are not adequately or accurately presented if they are only read about and discussed: these expressions should be seen, heard, felt, lived with if they are to be reestablished for us with any fidelity to the originals.

Hinduism has thousands of sacred texts that require Sanskrit, Tamil, Hindi, and other languages in order to analyze, interpret, and discuss them; yet many honored Hindu teachers tell us that Hinduism can get along quite well without any one of these texts, that a scholar who has the necessary linguistic skills and reads all the texts possible in a lifetime might still never have the faintest notion of what "Hinduism" is as a religion. In the study of Hinduism, perhaps more than is the case with any other religion, visual and audio resources are indispensable. Despite the ease of jet-age travel, it is still difficult for most of us to go to India; but films, slides, video, and audio materials can come to us and permit certain basic features of the religious life of India to declare themselves. Visual and audio materials cannot replace textual analysis, of course, any more than they can the necessary general reading, but in a remarkable way they do manage to put flesh on the bare bones of the classroom discussions or independent study.

Motion Pictures: Films, Video Resources, Videodiscs

Films

The members of the committee have screened many more films than are included in this listing, but could not, of course, see all the films which have been made on the subject of India. An earnest effort was made to cover those films which purport to treat Hinduism or its cultural manifestations at a level appropriate to the learning needs of mature users, and which are generally available to the public through purchase or lending arrangements. Films privately circulated and films designed for primary and secondary school audiences were not included. Even so, there is altogether an impressive number of films and videotapes which deserve critical attention.

The films are listed in three categories:

—films that are primarily concerned with some aspect of Hinduism as a Religious Tradition
—films that demonstrate certain cultural manifestations of the faith or which provide pertinent Cultural Background for the Study of Hinduism
—films that are useful for revealing the growing dialogue between Hinduism and the West.

Within each category, the titles are listed alphabetically, and the films are described and evaluated with special concern for their relevance to classroom and independent study situations. There is a topical index for those films and videotapes (as well as slides and recordings) that yield clearly to immediate classification.

It is evident from the range and sophistication of the films listed here that the study of Hinduism need no longer rely on travelogues or on generalizing and misleading surveys. The recent burgeoning of monographic documentary films makes it possible to view Hinduism through the focus of richly detailed, well-researched, carefully edited and narrated cinematographic productions. The potential of film monographs for independent learning and for teaching is increased enormously when they are accompanied by users' guides. Typical of the detailed studies are the materials produced by such expert Indologists as Fred Clothey, Joseph W. Elder, Clifford R. Jones, and H. Daniel Smith (and the videotape series by David M. Knipe, treated below)—all experienced academics familiar with the learning needs of students approaching Hinduism for serious exploration. Professor Clothey has examined, among other things, the Murugan cult of South India, widely celebrated there but generally ignored elsewhere; his three monographic film studies illuminate the lively admixture of popular folk practices with Brahminic traditions in this important regional cult. In the South Asia Film Series, each of Professor Elder's carefully designed film monographs presents a specific phenomenon for detailed examination, against a background skillfully portrayed.

Professor Jones's series, Art and Ritual in South India, shows traditional Hindu ritual in Kerala with special attention to the role of music
and dance in religious ceremonies. Professor Smith's *Image India, The
Hindu Way*, is a study of the Sri-Vaishnava Tengalai Brahmins of
Madras City, concentrating on ritual life in that community and
offering authentic insight into the ways ritual enters into the Hindu
way of life. As a genre, these film monographs provide much more
detail and depth than is possible in introductory, travelogue-type
films, and they permit the user to view selectively, rather than to be
forced to view broad vistas of Hinduism as presented in a generalized,
popular film. And almost without exception, the productions in these
series have users' guides to enhance their value to viewers, and to make
them more useful to seriously motivated independent learners.

A guide to the various series is provided in Appendix III. Using the
listings, reviews of individual titles can be located in the main body of
this volume.

When the review panel looked over the entire list of films and
videotapes discussed in this guide, it recognized that even though a
good number of useful films have been produced in the last decade,
many gaps remain. While materials for the study of regional Hinduism in Tamilnadu, Kerala, and Uttar Pradesh are beginning to be
available, other significant regions of Hindu India have been passed
over. With attention to ethnographic detail and a systematic approach
to regional and sectarian variations, we need to have films of popular
or folk Hinduism, as well as normative Brahminic rites; significant
rituals associated with a traditional orthoprax Hindu wedding;
studies of the almost infinite variety of women's rites; the universally
practiced placation rites of *arati* and related rituals; practices associated with the consecration of houses, temples, and images; agricultural
rites associated with planting and harvesting; studies of popular ways
of transmitting traditional values, such as devotional recitations of the
Ramayana and the educational function of temples and voluntary
associations; acts of devotion to saints, expecially to those holy persons
who are worshiped by significant segments of the population, such as
the Nayanmars and Alvars and other more recent lines of teachers and
ecstatics; religious practices at the major pilgrimage places and the
major festivals; and the religious significance of the various deities in
different parts of India.

Instructors have been developing highly effective techniques for
using visual resources as new materials have become available on film.
Further, the equipment for classroom use has been improved, and,
because of television, college students have become "visually literate."
Some teachers freely experiment with the film format as it comes to
them—showing only selected segments of a given film, or showing a
particularly demanding film twice, or projecting a film rich in visual
content, first without the sound track and later with the sound track.
Others supply their own commentary in replacement of the narration

they feel is inadequate or irrelevant to their course objectives. Some juxtapose two films depicting similar or different traditions to elicit discussion by students. Some make use of campus facilities for showing films out of class, often in informal settings, sometimes in carrels in libraries. Audio-visual materials in the hands of resourceful instructors have clearly become a stimulus to imaginative teaching.

It is ironic that just when there has been an increase in the quantity and quality of film resources, and their imaginative use, the availability of films has diminished markedly because of budget cuts for instructional purposes. Far too many administrators, and some instructors, still think classroom films are dispensable frills, not recognizing that they are as necessary as the printed page or the traditional lecture for the study of the religious ways of mankind.

Video Resources

While film materials have increased in quantity and quality in the last ten years, video resources for the study of Hinduism are still in an embryonic stage. Any film can readily be converted to video, and a number of distributors now offer both video and film versions for sale. For this reason, in our alphabetical evaluation both film and video resources are listed together rather than separately. The evaluation panel is aware that however practical the merging of these two mediums may be, it scarcely does justice to the potential of video for transmitting images of India.

The videocassette, like a medium-sized book but lighter in weight, is much simpler and quieter to operate than a film, and it has all the fast-forward, reverse, and pause capacities of audio tapes. This is of enormous consequence to the independent learner unfamiliar with movie projection equipment, and adapts well to small, informal study groups. Yet the videocassette is not limited to solitary viewers or to intimate groups. While a single monitor suffices for a small class, linked monitors producing the same picture from a single cassette in a single player can be arranged for larger classes. Many universities now have "media" lecture halls with television monitors stationed between every fourth and fifth row at each side of the hall.

Because of their flexibility for use in different situations, their relatively simple operation by inexperienced users, and the increasing utilization being made of them by anthropologists, sociologists, historians of religions, and others who take video cameras into the field and the studio to produce new video documents geared to the small screen medium, it is safe to predict that growing numbers of institutions as well as private individuals will consider assembling video-cassette libraries. In schools and colleges, this makes possible the deployment of carrels equipped for independent learning, with video-cassette monitors, audio equipment, slide projectors, and even micro-fiche readers. New video resources, including standard films and slide sets transferred to videocassettes, tape-slide presentations, music and chants, and archival materials can be made conveniently accessible in these carrels, and incorporated as regular assignments by instructors, liberating class sessions for discussion and other instructional strategies. Similar carrels can be placed in public libraries, in museums, in religious institutions, and even—on a smaller, more informal, scale—in homes. For, clearly, those who wish to learn at their own pace, by watching a segment or a program or a series in the convenient videocassette format, are not limited to the role of a conventionally matriculated student enrolled in a typical classroom course. At present, however, the major utilization of videocassettes is by teachers in educational programs who refer students to videocassette resources at the outset of a course in order to move the class quickly to an advanced level, or to encourage independent study by students with special interests by referring them to resources available when formal courses of relevant study are not available.

Thus far, the only substantial contribution to the study of Hinduism that employs video's potential for independent learning is the videocassette series produced by Professor David M. Knipe, *Exploring the Religions of South India*, with nine of the fifteen programs devoted to Hindu phenomena. This low-budget but imaginative and pioneer effort utilizes for the series films made in India, 1157 slides, and numerous paintings, sculptures, and ritual artifacts to illustrate discussions of the essential features of Hinduism. In another less technologically advanced videocassette series, *Psyche and Symbol* (ten presentations of what are essentially classroom slide-lectures by Joseph Campbell), there is one program on Kundalini Yoga. Both of these series have been, and no doubt will continue to be, broadcast regionally to television audiences on educational networks. But their primary circulation will occur in videocassette form in universities, public schools, museums, public libraries, religious institutions, and eventually in private homes. Approximately forty colleges and universities in the United States, Canada, and Australia are now using the videocassette series, *Exploring the Religions of South Asia*, to supplement or structure courses in Asian or world religions, or to spotlight specific dimensions of one religion such as Hinduism. (There is nothing on Hinduism to match the scale of Japan: *The Living Tradition*, the sixteen-unit video course with study guide and texts produced by Edwin O. Reischauer with Jackson Bailey through the University of Mid-America with a budget of one-and-a-half million dollars, and access to the television and film resources of the NHK network in Japan.)

Videodiscs

Just when audio-video carrels and cassette libraries are being established as vital new dimensions of our educational institutions, an entirely new advance may be forthcoming in media technology—the videodisc. Introduced by a number of companies using incompatible technologies, videodiscs have the capacity to replace films, slides, videotapes and even the printed page for many educational purposes. Although the eventual spread of the videodisc will take several years, this area is well worth watching. The videodisc is to videotape what microfiche is to books. A disc which is much like a phonograph record and costs under $10.00 when mass-produced, is played on a turntable expected to market for under $500.00, the latter being plugged into a standard television set. The player utilizes a micro-power laser beam to pick up and transmit from a single disc 54,000 separate images—i.e., 54,000 color slides (ten times as many as are currently available on India), or 54,000 pages of text (ten years each of ten academic journals), fifteen hours of audio material, or thirty minutes of film or video material. A remarkable capacity of the MCA-Philips system (but not the RCA) is that of retrieving by index dial and freeze-framing any one of the 54,000 images, as well as placing in slow motion forward or reverse any film or video sequence. In a few years, these systems may well be in our homes, departmental offices, university libraries, and public institutions. They will be remarkably inexpensive considering their value and versatility. One cannot but be impressed with the thought of a videodisc library of instructional film, video, slide, and audio materials, easily stored, ineradicable, any segment of which can be located and transmitted for teaching, research, or independent learning.

Still Photos: Slides & Filmstrips, and Microfiche

Slides and Filmstrips

The committee also reviewed for evaluation a number of commercially available slide sets and filmstrips. Generally, the subject matter of these fell naturally into the same three categories as did the films: materials designed primarily for the presentation of Hinduism as a Religious Tradition; materials relevant to the study of the Cultural Background of Hinduism; and materials deriving from the dialogue between Hinduism and the West. The first category represents sets of still shots depicting ceremonies in the temple and at home, festivals, pilgrimage sites and practices associated therewith; yogic postures and gestures used in meditation and related spiritual and bodily disciplines; and deities pictured in sculpture and painting. Often such materials were accompanied by useful printed guides. The second category contains sets of photographs of artistic monuments, archeological sites, theatrical performances, and village life. Often designed for special audiences—viz., art historians, archeologists, ethnologists or anthropologists—these resources nevertheless are also relevant to the needs of an interdisciplinary approach to the study of Hinduism; such users' guides as are furnished with these sets were deemed helpful, more or less, to the instructor or independent learner focusing on Hinduism. Materials in this category often presuppose considerable background in the study of Hinduism. The third category boasts only a few sets at the time of this review, namely those produced and distributed by the U.S.-based ISKCON (the "Hare Krishna Movement"). The available slide sets are reviewed immediately following the film reviews in the three respective categories.

Given the marked preference by many instructors for slides, it is surprising that there are not more sets targeted to the needs of their specific classroom presentations or produced for the design of topically focused, independent learning packages. There are few, if any, monographic sets of slides available; here the production of slide resources has not kept pace with the creation of cinematographic studies. Hence, those who depend exclusively on slides are faced with limitations: the resources do not exist—or have not yet been made commercially available—for the in-depth study of a particular Hindu phenomenon or the localized expression of a cult. Yet to many instructors, however precise and scholarly may be recently available cinematic resources, the use of films in their own instructional programs remains unwieldy, intrusive, and impractical.

Films and slides perform different functions. While films can represent action and give the viewer a sense approximating that of a participant in the filmed event, motion pictures generally cannot be stopped for special consideration of a frame. To do so breaks the continuity; films are programmed for action and pace, and they are normally intended to be shown without interruption. Slides, by contrast, not only permit but invite expanded explanation of visual details and discussion of various concepts or activities related to the subject shown. Further, slide sets may be utilized, at the instructor's discretion, to show only the most pertinent visual data, facilitating omission of irrelevant views. Hence, to many instructors slides adapt more flexibly to their classroom or independent learning programs.

Some instructors use fixed visual images very sparingly and with great discrimination—displaying only four or five, or a dozen or so, slides in a single presentation to fit the topic under consideration; a few instructors with rear-projection facilities are known to leave a single picture—of a temple, of a sacred site, or a consecrated image, of a mystical symbol, or of a ritual moment—on-screen for an entire class period, while the lecture or discussion evolves, in order to impress that picture firmly in the minds of the students. Other instructors use the same facilities to project an ever-changing array of images, heavily loading their presentations with visual cues of many kinds. Because mechanics are less obtrusive (especially if the projector is enclosed in a booth to eliminate the sound, while the controls remain at the lecturn), the projection of a tray of slides, carefully selected ahead of time, provides an experienced instructor with easy visual clues for sophisticated lectures with but infrequent reference to notes. Many instructors find that slides are easily adapted to their own style of teaching. Finally, in a time of an endemic "budget crunch," judiciously purchased slide sets, obtained for permanent acquisition through special instructional or library budgets, seem more practical to those with limited funds than the perennial quest for discretional monies to secure films on a repeated rental basis.

Of course, were minimal acquisition costs the only factor to consider, filmstrips would be the obvious solution for visual enrichment of instructional programs. But filmstrips present problems unique to the very format which permits their low cost. Because they are pictures programmed onto a roll of 35mm color film, the order of the pictures determined by the producer of the filmstrip must be followed. It is both difficult and distracting to skip around since the intervening frames must be passed. While most secondary schools use filmstrips regularly in their instructional programs, college instructors rarely do. Hence, the equipment required for using filmstrips is not always available in college classrooms. And, most importantly, very few commercially available filmstrips are geared to college-level learning needs; by and large filmstrips are designed for and most pertinent to primary and secondary school learning levels. Nonetheless, some filmstrips have been noted in our list of slides. These appear to have some value, albeit limited, to college-level instructors and adult independent learners. And there are a few filmstrips cued to a tape or to a record which, to some, may provide ready-made illustrated lectures whether employed in classroom or study-carrel.

The evaluation panel was impressed by the sheer numbers of slides and filmstrips available. As such, these should offer a major resource for the study of Hinduism or for learning about Hinduism's cultural setting. In addition to the commercially available visuals, it is widely known that many professional Indologists who teach courses on Hinduism possess what amounts collectively to a vast archive of photographs which, if more easily accessible to other instructors, could supplement materials currently on the market. An effort to bridge the availability gap was made some years ago in the "India-Hinduism" set, promoted by Professor Charles Kennedy with the assistance of the American Academy of Religion as part of the Asian Religions Media Resources Catalogue. In addition to this one set on Hinduism, the project also made available sets of slides on other Asian religious traditions. Further efforts along these lines, at least as relates to Hinduism, might be undertaken, with special attention to the production of monographic slide sets.

Microfiche
Each 4" by 6" microfiche plastic card can provide immense quantities of information, is cheap to produce, is easily stored and retrieved, is very durable, and, when used with a viewer, can be projected for easy reading. Microfiche can reproduce anything that can be photo-

graphed: manuscripts, books, documents, pictures, charts, maps. Microfiche retrieval systems have been developed that are compatible with computer technology. Most libraries now provide microfiche viewers and can give information about microfiche resources. Microfiche is especially useful for providing copies of materials that would not otherwise be available, and for independent study. For classroom use the resolution of projected microfiche is not as good as with slides, and if not projected a viewer must be provided for each student.

A massive microfiche program has been undertaken by the American Committee for South Asian Art in collaboration with the Inter Documentation Company in Switzerland, a major source for microfiche materials. As well, the Institute for the Advanced Study of World Religions at the State University of New York, Stony Brook, has duplicated a complete set of the Sanskrit manuscripts from the University of Pennsylvania and extensive materials on Buddhism. The Institute has duplicating facilities for microfiche, and helps scholars secure copies of rare books and manuscripts, charging actual costs for their services. In addition to these programs, the Association for Asian Studies, South Asia Microform Project, has been reproducing materials for archival purposes for some time now. Also, the University of Chicago Press has experimented with publishing in microfiche.

Clearly, the use of microfiche for preparing materials to use in the study of Hinduism has not yet been fully exploited.

Recorded Sound: Records and Audio Tapes

It is difficult to imagine that any non-Indian could have a sense of what Hinduism means to a Hindu without an awareness of the roles that music and chanting play in the religious life and thought of Hindus. What is required is not merely an intellectual awareness but a familiar appreciation, gained through repeated attentive listening, of the chanting of the Vedas; the singing of devotional hymns; the meditative instrumental music, such as that of the vina, the sitar, and the flute, expressing praise, longing, and awe; the closeness to the natural world revealed in the rhythms, the morning and evening ragas, the music for the rites of passage; the joyous and instructive kirtanas and bhajanas. This is highly sophisticated religious music, requiring sophisticated listening lest the subtleties be missed. At its best, Hindu religious music is not a background sound effect for rituals nor a device for manipulating emotions, but is religious aspiration and insight fittingly expressed in reflective, tonal, and rhythmic modes.

Fortunately, within the past quarter of a century a considerable number of recordings of Hindu religious music have become available in the West, making it possible for anyone seriously interested in understanding Hinduism to study and become familiar with some of the many kinds of music that are a part of the everyday life of the Hindu.

In the classroom, the students can be introduced to carefully selected, illustrative passages which may be repeated often enough to get past the initial sense of strangeness. For independent learning the records may be utilized in study carrels or played at home. The recordings mentioned in this guide are but a *very* few selected from a much larger number currently available, and represent those which have remained in stock with leading distributors over the past several years and which will probably remain available from the same reliable sources for some time to come. Whenever possible, the date of the actual recording has been noted. The lists in each of the three sections of our reviews, provide a beginning from which it is possible to explore some of the music traditions associated with Hinduism.

In addition to musical selections, notice has also been given to four or five recordings which feature chants or recitations of sacred texts. There is an obvious need for more learning resources when it comes to the spoken word, so central to the tradition of Hindu education and piety. The two albums of Vedic chanting already available may be sufficient for most instructors offering introductory surveys of the Hindu religious tradition, but more advanced students will find the selections wanting. It may require special future projects to provide serviceable renderings of the *Ramayana* and of the *Bhagavad Gita* for students studying these texts, whether in translation, in the original Sanskrit, or in vernacular versions. And, there is still not enough available to capture the sounds of the poetic utterances typical of regional bhakti movements, the present resources being very limited, indeed.

From time to time taped lectures by, or interviews with, luminous English-speaking Hindu figures have been made available. The very nature of such recordings makes many of these productions of transitory historical interest at best; however, addresses and homilies by such personalities as Gandhi, Radhakrishnan, and other famous persons are preserved in audio archives in the United States, Canada, Great Britain, and India. Even though some instructors feel that recorded messages, especially lectures by voices unfamiliar to their students, are of limited pedagogical value, the need continues for procurement and dissemination to interested parties of the spoken word so that the views of contemporary exponents and interpreters of Hinduism as a living faith may be heard by new generations in classrooms and study carrels. In addition to the commercial and other suppliers of recorded materials listed in Appendix I and Appendix II of this guide, interested readers are reminded of the retrieval potential of the audio archives of the Library of Congress, the New York Public Library, and at Stanford, Syracuse, Toronto, and Yale universities.

A Postscript to Buyers/Distributors/Producers of Films and Other Learning Resources

This guide represents an attempt to alert instructors in the classroom and adults using independent learning resources to what is available and, among the available materials, to recommend what appears to be most useful. The criteria invoked for evaluating the materials reviewed become apparent in the descriptions and comments attached to each entry in our list. In retrospect, members of the panel feel some discoveries were made in the course of the project which should be made explicit to those who purchase, distribute, and produce films and other learning resources. While what we say will come as no surprise to professionals in educational technology and learning resources supply services, still their articulation here may have some force.

Perhaps the most significant conviction to impress the panel as it emerges from this review is that there is, indeed, an audience for college-level or adult-targeted learning resources. The needs of sophisticated, visually literate, and intellectually discriminating users should not be overlooked when planning purchase or production of materials. Among those who may wish to learn more about a religion or culture other than their own are not only college-level students, ranging in age from their late teens to their mid-seventies, but also independent learners of all kinds—retired persons seeking personal enrichment, professionals preparing themselves for foreign-area assignments, members of voluntary study groups (churches and synagogues, civic or fraternal organizations) who select materials for learning units, and independent learners in more or less formal, credit or non-credit, "college without walls" programs. The needs of such potential customers—whether they do their work on a college campus, in a public library, at a local museum or historical society, at home via closed circuit television, or independently—are different from and more demanding than those of people who use materials produced for mass market consumption. The demands for materials to suit the needs of mature learners is likely to increase rather than diminish in coming years.

It may also be worth noting the trend toward, and the positive response to, "monographic" studies of things Hindu and Indian. One of the members of the screening panel observed some years ago that we already had all the encyclopedic, "once-over-lightly," panoramic surveys of Hinduism we need—whether they be book or non-book resources; what is needed is more focused and in-depth, monographic studies of particular phenomena of Hinduism, or of regional expressions of Hinduism, to illuminate specific manifestations of the tradition. Yet the 20- to 30-minute generalizations treating "Hinduism" continue to find favor among those planning purchases and/or production of new film resources. Granted that there will always be a ready audience for the compact presentations of intro-

ductory or review approaches to a tradition; it is this panel's hope that
this recognition will be balanced by a practical response to what
pertains to the target needs of mature and informed users.

Time and again the panelists found themselves impressed by the
importance of "Users' Guides" with films, slides, and filmstrips. This
discovery, too, deserves candid affirmation. Almost invariably the
well-written, carefully documented guide—as distinguished from an
uncritical blurb—increases immensely the uses to which a resource
may be put in the hands of an intelligent viewer. While distribution of
printed materials with audio-visual rentals can, admittedly, become a
formidable problem involving additional labor and reprinting ex-
penditures, the guide promotes a wider use and enhances immeasur-
ably the value of the audio-visual materials as aids to learning. The
panel wrestled with, but did not fully resolve, the following important
questions: who should write the users' guide to a film or slide set? to
whom should the guide be addressed? should a guide identify every
ambiguous visual? should guides contain "discussion questions"?
how extensive should be recommendations for further readings?

The panel also observed that the length of a film was almost always
independent of the quality of reporting or of the authenticity of
content. Mass-audience films seem quite regularly to aim at a length
compatible with commercial broadcasting segments (27 to 28 minutes,
or half, or twice that time). In too many cases the reviewers found that
this artificial imposition of length involved senseless padding, insertion of dazzling but mindless visual effects, and incorporating imaginative but meaningless studio shots or irrelevant footage. By contrast,
the panel recommended films of anywhere from 8 or 9 minutes to 45
minutes. The evaluation, quite obviously, had to do with pedagogical
dependability of the documentary, not with its length. Aside from that
sine qua non, the only concern most instructors might be expected to
have in regard to the length of a film is that in a classroom session, it
allow ample time for contextual references to matters already covered
in course work and for a class discussion after the film is viewed.

Panelists also reflected in retrospect that it was not ordinarily the
high-budget, glossy, "well-made" documentary film that garnered
their praise. The documentaries, slide sets, and other learning resources which most consistently found favor with these reviewers were
those which, while camerawork and certain technical phases of
production were normally left to professional cimematographers,
involved the expertise of content specialists and/or experienced
classroom teachers who had over a period of some years continually
dealt with Hinduism as an academic adventure. Some of the best
resources presently available were done on a "shoe-string" budget,
with "cutting ratios" of 3:1, even 2:1, or less. These resulted from
projects in which a sole scholar thoroughly familiar with the material
went out into the field with one Indian cameraman, returning with
raw footage of incalculable pedagogic worth. This is not to say that

such productions are faultless, nor that they could not have been considerably improved at all stages by consultation with skilled "media specialists," or technically enhanced by utilization of sophisticated equipment such as is written into the generous budgets of more amply endowed projects. Consequently, the panel would urge that in future production projects more serious thought be given to implementing from the very beginning a reciprocal working collaboration between professional media experts and the content specialists with classroom experience. Such a reciprocal working collaboration should be fostered at other project stages as well: too often films are stocked at libraries or acquired by institutions through audio-visual purchasing agents only on the basis of promotional materials circulated by distributors or on the recommendations published for media specialists by other media specialists. All too rarely is advice or opinion sought from the experienced instructor who, in addition to providing a perspective based on field trips to India, is a content expert intimately familiar with the educational needs and goals of students in the classroom or study carrel.

The present critical list may provide the first clear evidence for those who plan, produce, distribute, and purchase films and other learning resources of just what expectations classroom specialists have for learning resources focusing on Hinduism. The present statement, by way of a "Postscript" to this project, may also be the first time a call for collaboration has been issued, an invitation that is more poignant for being so long overdue.

1

Hinduism as a Religious Tradition

Films and Videotapes

Altar of Fire
 45 minutes, color, 16mm, 1977
 Sale $600.00, (video $420.00), Rental $35.00
 Robert Gardner and Frits Staal
 Extension Media Center
 University of California—Berkeley
 Berkeley, CA 94720
 Also available from UIll

This important film presents in rich detail and splendid cinematography a 3,000-year-old Vedic ritual performed in a Kerala village in 1975 by Nambudiri brahmans. It was made possible through the dedicated cooperation of Indian, American, and European scholars and the remnant but still vital Vedic ritualists of southwestern India. The Nambudiri brahmans reconstructed, said to be for the last time, the ancient Vedic rite of the agnicayana, "the piling of the fire-altar." It may not be the "world's oldest surviving ritual" as the guide proclaims (one thinks of the North Asian bear rites, certain shamanic rites, and others), but to watch this film unfold the details of this twelve-day rite, involving the constant activity of seventeen priests and the sacrificer himself, the production of the vast bird-shaped altar out of more than a thousand bricks, the preparation and performances of the sacrificer, the soma rituals, and the dramatic kindling of Agni himself, is to enter an archaic spiritual legacy as if transported to a long-gone era. With an extraordinary blend of sophistication and primordiality, the ritual presents itself with unforgettable impact. Above all, the power of the oral tradition resounds throughout this religious drama.

Comments: This Vedic ritual has miraculously survived into the modern age as one of the great spiritual creations of mankind, comparable to other treasures of religious art, architecture, literature, and music. This is the first available film to portray the significance of the Vedic heritage. Two black-and-white predecessors, Professor Staal's *Vedic Ritual in South India*, on the upanayana and preparations for sacrifice, and Professor van Buitenen's excellent *Vajapeya*, another soma rite filmed during its reconstructed performance in Poona in 1955, have not been available for rental or purchase. *Altar of Fire* is therefore a tour de force, but one that requires careful preparation on the part of the instructor or independent student. The major shortcoming of the film is the lack of discussion of the basis of the *agnicayana* in the central Vedic mythology. Therefore, the film is recommended for advanced students who have read at least an introductory work on Vedic religion. A brief guide is available now, and Professor Staal is preparing a book on the ritual (to be published in the early 1980s, as well as an accompanying set of records.

The Avatar: Concept and Example
  25 minutes, color, 16mm & videotape, 1977
  Sale $450.00, Rental $45.00
  Robert A. McDermott and Nuala O'Faolain—Man's Religious Quest
  Media Guild
  118 South Acacia
  Solona Beach, CA 92075

As the title indicates, this film explores the concept of the avatar in the Hindu tradition, with dual focus on a traditional exemplar, Krishna, and the contemporary figure, Sri Aurobindo. Utilizing the *Bhagavad Gita*, the first third of the film treats Krishna as the Divine Spirit present on earth and as "restorer of dharma." The remaining two-thirds of the film turns to the figure of Aurobindo, explains his teaching in regard to the avatar concept, and advances the claims made for his status as avatar of the present age. The film makes use of animated diagrams to depict aspects of Aurobindo's thought, and records statements by leading British disciples of Aurobindo. The concluding footage shows the Aurobindo Ashram at Pondicherry in South India and the nearby utopian city of Auroville.

Comments: This film was made by The Open University, Great Britain, for students enrolled in a course on world religions, and presupposes familiarity with writings by and about Aurobindo through a series of assigned readings. Others using the film will find it more intelligible if they are similarly acquainted with Aurobindo's teaching and mission. The general approach to the concept of avatar in this film is limited, on the one hand, to the doctrine enunciated in the *Bhagavad Gita* and, on the other, to the person of Aurobindo as hypostasized by his devotees. For a traditional interpretation of the Hindu concept of avatara, see below, *Sectarian Hinduism: Lord Vishnu and His Worship.* Professor McDermott's booklet *Modern Hinduism: Gandhi and Aurobindo*, which was written to accompany this film, is published in England by The Open University Press.

Consecration of a Temple
  25 minutes, color, 16mm, 1979
  Sale $125.00, Rental $17.00
  Fred Clothey, Worldview Productions
  Department of South Asian Studies
  1242 Van Hise Hall
  University of Wisconsin—Madison
  Madison, WI 53706

The commendably spare narration of this excellent film begins: "A traditional Hindu temple is being built in Pittsburgh—one of the first orthodox temples in America—and is being dedicated to the god Venkateshwara, an important South Indian deity." The opening shots are of the flagpole being raised by imported Indian artisans dressed in dhotis, assisted by American construction workers in jeans. Thereupon follows documentation of the major steps observed during the five-day consecration rituals: performing the elaborate fire sacrifices, installing the images of guardian figures, placing the golden finial atop the temple dome, pouring sanctified water over the structure, paying ritual respect to the now-consecrated temple, bathing the main image within the inner shrine, decorating the main image, and distributing "prasada" offered first to the deity then only to the faithful devotees who have gathered for the momentous occasion.

Comments: Throughout, various technicalities of Hindu temple worship are explained in context, using a minimum of non-English terms, stressing all the while the utilization in the consecration rites of such elements as fire, water, food offerings, and the spoken word in Sanskrit. The film contains some brief but good shots of artisans at work, priests exercising their sacerdotal functions, dignitaries providing pomp to the proceedings, a dancer (Roxanne Gupta) performing a Bharata Natyam offering in the vestibule area, and scores of worshipers more or less involved in the proceedings. Several adult witnesses are interviewed on-camera (including Professor V. Narayana Rao of the University of Wisconsin), as well as two American-born Indian schoolgirls; all seem to stress in their responses the importance of the temple's presence in America for the younger generation of Indo-Americans.

While the film inadvertantly gives the impression that Hindu temple worship is a congregational experience—in fact the narration mentions the importance of a sense of communion with others during worship—it nonetheless provides a rare glimpse of authentic procedures of worship in a Hindu temple setting. Some maps or charts or other means of orienting the viewer to the temple site would have been helpful, but such may be available in the forthcoming guide and/or by writing to the temple authorities (Sri Venkateswara Temple, Penn Hills, 1620 Branning Road, Pittsburgh, PA 15235). This film will probably find a valued place in many classrooms. It may also be confidently used, pending issue of a suitable study guide, for independent learning by those who wish to familiarize themselves with the steps of consecration rites and/or with the elements used in Hindu temple worship.

A Contemporary Guru: Rajnish
  30 minutes, color, ¾" videocassette, 1975
  Sale $45.00
  David Knipe—Exploring the Religions of South Asia
  Department of South Asian Studies
  1242 Van Hise Hall
  University of Wisconsin—Madison
  Madison, WI 53706

This film provides a useful insight into one of the many contemporary personality cults of India by furnishing vignettes of its leading figure, Rajnish, interspersed with statements elicited from some of his devoted disciples. The stated aim of the presentation is to examine the role of the guru and the place of ecstasy and possession in the process of an individual's religious transformation. Most of the filmed footage has as its setting Rajnish's ashram in Poona. There Rajnish is recorded preaching in English to an assembly of Indian and European devotees, and the camera notes some of the many techniques recommended by the spiritual master for "becoming One." The practice of cultivating ecstasy through movement, by dancing and whirling, is vividly portrayed at a group gathering; there are a number of shots of devotees in trance while other, less dramatic forms of "dynamic meditation" are also shown. The honor accorded to the person of Rajnish, in addition to the reverence paid to his portraits and symbols, provides eloquent testimony to the phenomenon of guru-bhakti, an enduring presence in popular Hinduism and a phenomenon to which this videocassette presentation affords a memorable introduction. A late sequence contains an interview with a follower who has founded a Rajnish Center in Australia.

  Comments: This is a clear, coherent, and visually effective presentation. It may be used profitably as an introduction to the non-rational dimension of spiritual discipline; it contains good footage of devotees in ecstasy. The film may also have specific topical interest for many viewers due to the growing numbers of Europeans and Americans who are becoming disciples of Rajnish. For films on related topics, see the Topical Index under Ecstasy, Personality Cults, etc. [Note: a feature-length film, *Bhagwan,* by Robert Hillman on Rajnish was produced in 1978 by Michael Wiese Films; no further details available at press time.]

Death and Rebirth in Hinduism
    30 minutes, color, ¾″ videocassette, 1975
    Sale $45.00
    David M. Knipe—Exploring the Religions of South Asia
    Department of South Asian Studies
    1242 Van Hise Hall
    University of Wisconsin—Madison
    Madison, WI 53706

". . . If there is anything that ties together the great religious traditions of India . . . it is the unshakable belief in transmigration, a belief that birth, youth, old age, death, rebirth succeed one another in a process. . . ." So observes Professor David M. Knipe near the beginning of this presentation. He moves beyond this range of concern almost immediately to focus on that complex of hopes, ideas, and practices reflecting the trust that the seemingly inexorable process can be halted—if not once and for all, at least temporarily. Death rites and funerary practices of Hinduism reflect this trust most clearly inasmuch as the rituals seem to be aimed at staving off redeath of the departed person in an afterlife. After a brief discussion of the vocabulary associated with death/rebirth in Hinduism (karma, samsara, moksha, dharma), the bulk of the presentation is given over to a review of cremation (antyeshti) and postmortem memorial (shraddha) rites, drawing examples from various areas of rural and urban Indian practices.

Comments: It should be clearly understood by potential viewers of this program that the reference to "rebirth" in the title is only an allusion to the ideological structure that gives poignancy and dimension to the death rites and memorial celebrations so punctiliously performed, and which provide the main emphasis of the study. It should also be noted that this program was designed to be used to complement another in the same series, *The Life Cycle in Hinduism: Birth, Initiation, Marriage,* (q.v.), dealing with other life-cycle celebrations. Because this presentation is rich in detail and represents an in-depth treatment of a specialized topic—death and funerary rites—it may have a variety of uses both for the independent learner and the classroom student. It provides a suggestive, open-ended approach to the complex topic both in its Hindu setting and in the larger framework of a history of religions approach to such matters as death and eschatology. For other treatments of related topics, see the Topical Index under Ancestral Offerings, Death, etc.

Floating in the Air, Followed by the Wind
    34 minutes, color, 16mm, 1974
    Sale $390.00, Rental $15.25

Michigan State University College of Human Medicine—Biological Communications
Audio-Visual Center
Indiana University
Bloomington, IN 47401
Also available from UCB, IndU, BYU, UWash

Shot in Kuala Lumpur, Malaysia, by a medical research team, this film presents several young devotees of the Hindu god Murugan with metal spears stuck in their flesh as they carry a heavy peacock-adorned construction. The film depicts elaborate preparation for the trance state necessary for this grueling act of devotion. Led by the guru (fakir), the devotees dance into a trance state and then allow a small spear to pierce their tongues. The film shows many scenes of trances, insertions of spears during these trance states, and an interesting view of the guru's eleven-year-old son with a spear in his tongue during an ecstatic dance. The guru carries a sixty-pound "peacock"—arrows and spears dug deep into his chest and back with no apparent ill effect. Interviews with this boy and other ecstatics reveal the range of the devotees' motives for their vows; the participants offer fascinating accounts of their ecstatic experiences.

Comments: This film is extraordinary, both visually and conceptually. It effectively shows the power of the Murugan cult, and its ability to sustain the rigors of such demanding ecstatic practices. There is careful attention given to the spiritual-psychological preparations necessary for these devotions. The background music is effective and the script is informative, although the impact of the film is marred by a few mispronunciations and a few inaudible words. It may well supplement the more general film *Murugan*, and the films on Murugan temple ritual—*Pankuni Uttaram. . . , Skanda-Sasti. . . ,* and *Yakam . . . (q.v.).*

Four Holy Men: Renunciation in Hindu Society
37 minutes, color, 16mm, 1976
Sale $160.00, Rental $20.00
Mira Reym Binford, Michael Camerini, Joseph Elder
University of Wisconsin—Contemporary South Asian Film series
Department of South Asian Studies
1242 Van Hise Hall
University of Wisconsin—Madison
Madison, WI 53706
Also available from WashSt

The film begins with man-on-the street interviews of ordinary people in India answering questions on whether there are true holy men (sadhus) in India and what their place in society is or should be. The lives of four purportedly holy men are portrayed to illustrate the range of lifestyles encompassed by this ideal in contemporary India. The people shown are: (1) a follower of the Ramakrishna sect, devoting his life to service in a Ramakrishna Mission hospital; (2) the head of a traditional Indian monastery; (3) a sannyasin (recluse); and (4) a scholar-activist in a Hindu-oriented political party.

Comments: The opinions expressed by those interviewed in the film are interesting, varied, and intelligible. The lifestyles portrayed are indeed within the Hindu norms of meritorious religious existence, without reaching the extremes we have been led to expect of Mahatmas and avatars, yogins and gurus on the banks of the Ganges. The film is a good starting point for discussions of religion in India, and an antidote for those who identify Hinduism with personality cults focused on jet-set yogis. By recording the speakers in vernacular languages, with English subtitles, this film provides an immediacy which is rare in educational films. The guide for this film, as for all of the films in the University of Wisconsin series, ranks with the best in the field.

Four Religions (Part I and Part II)
    60 minutes, b/w, 16mm, 1961
    Sale $595.00, Rental $60.00
    James Beveridge and Arnold Toynbee
    Benchmark Films, Inc.
    145 Scarborough Road
    Briarcliff Manor, NY 10510
    Also available from UAriz, FlaSt, USoFla, NoILL, UILL, IndU, UMe, BU, UMinn, SyrU, KentSt, BYU, UWisc

With the aid of an interview with Arnold Toynbee, this film explores the similarities and differences between Hinduism, Buddhism, Islam, and Christianity. Although the film shows some of the dissimilarities of beliefs, practices, and institutions of these religious traditions, Professor Toynbee nevertheless argues that all religions reveal an underlying unity of aim and effect. In addition to the full sixty-minute version, this film is also available in two parts: "I. Hinduism and Buddhism"; "II. Christianity and Islam." The fifteen-minute Hinduism section, which is available separately, includes shots of the Indus Valley, religious practices in Banaras, yoga practice, temple worship, and groups of workers. It also explains the cow as a symbol of peace, and in the interview with Professor Toynbee, stresses the "tolerance of Hinduism."

Comments: This film is partly misleading and has been superseded by recent treatments such as those cited in the Topical Index.

The Goddess Bhagavati: Art and Ritual in South India
  15 minutes, color, 16mm, 1976
  Clifford Jones—Traditional Art & Ritual in South India
  Inquire: Clifford Jones, South Asia Center,
  School of International Affairs
  Columbia University
  New York, N.Y. 10027

This depicts the ritualized construction of an image of the goddess Bhagavati, using powders in five colors on a mandala upon the floor. This art is preserved in the Ambalavasi community of Kerala, where the film was made. In the course of the film, the importance of art in ritual is discussed, and the musical and tantric ritual accompaniment to the rite is shown. The film includes the important steps in making the room-sized image—tracing the mandala upon the floor, calculating the proportions of the image, filling in the five ritually significant colors, making the breasts of the goddess with mounds of rice, and ritually awakening her with a mirror before the eyes. A Nayar "shaman" priest performs an ecstatic dance with ritual sword, reaching a trance state in communication with the goddess.

Comments: This is a vivid and colorful film with good cinematography and narration. However, the viewer should be forewarned that the subject matter and contents of the film are difficult and require considerable pedagogical support. The filmmaker, Professor Jones, considers this film to be preparatory to *The Worship of the Deity Ayyapanan . . .* and *The Serpent Deities . . .*, which are in the same series. In fact, seeing the three together helps answer some of the questions raised in each.

Himalayan Shaman: Northern Nepal
Himalayan Shaman: Southern Nepal
  14 minutes, color, 16mm, 1968
  Sale $175.00, Rental $9.00
  John and Patricia Hitchock
  International Film Bureau, Inc.
  332 South Michigan Avenue
  Chicago, IL 60604
  Also available from ArizSt, UCB, UCt, Boise, BU, SyrU, PennSt, UUtah

These two films by anthropologists show healing shamans at work—the first in northern Nepal going about his tasks with great eclat in costume, and using his body as a medium for several spirits; the second in southern and more Hinduized Nepal approaching his work by combining local traditions and spells with what he saw done in an army hospital during World War II, as well as with what he had learned from Tibetan lore and Hindu Ayurvedic practices. Neither film is explicit about the Hindu context of these folk specialists, but both mention caste and/or untouchability.

Comments: These are fascinating vignettes of village-level medical practices, affording insights as to how magic rites and marginally religious specialists combine to present a revealing picture of "popular," "folk" traditions in action. Both films consistently avoid technical language, which is an asset for wide-spectrum audience appeal but a liability for those who would like to know more about specifics. The Northern film is tighter in focus, with an excellent portrayal of the archaic shaman's ecstatic dance and his relation to the community. The Southern film lacks information on the history of shamanism in relation to the indigenous religious life, as well as the roles of the shamans in traditional major religions at the village level.

Hindu Devotions at Dawn
    10 minutes, color, 16mm, 1969
    Sale $110.00, Rental $10.00
    H. Daniel Smith—Image India
    Film Marketing Division/Film Rental Library
    Syracuse University
    1455 East Colvin Street
    Syracuse, NY 13210
    Also available from UWash, UWisc

A middle-aged Sri-Vaishnava Tengalai brahman man in Madras is shown in his daily morning worship. He applies his sectarian marks, orients himself in sacred space and time, relates himself to the deities and the elements, and recites the sacred gayatri mantra.

Comments: The narration of this film is not descriptive; instead, Professor Smith accomplishes effectively a recapitulation of the devotee's thoughts during his devotional practices. The simplicity and power of personal piety in Hinduism are well articulated in what might otherwise be dismissed by the outsider as a routine and colorless operation. Professor Smith's film is readily intelligible to all levels of viewers and a user's guide is available on request. For a different treatment of the same ritual, see Srinivasan's *The Hindu Ritual Sandhya*, where the rites are shown performed in slightly different style by a man of a different sect.

Hindu Family Celebration: 60th Birthday
    9 minutes, color, 16mm, 1969
    Sale $100.00, Rental $9.00

H. Daniel Smith—Image India
Film Marketing Division/Film Rental Library
Syracuse University
1455 East Colvin Street
Syracuse, NY 13210
Also available from UWash

Filmed in Madras among the Tengalai Sri-Vaishnavas, this colorful portrayal of a celebration honoring a man who has just completed his sixtieth year centers on an elaborate ritual setting. Together with his wife, and under the direction of the family priest, the sacrificer makes fire offerings, undergoes a ritual bath, renews his marriage vows, and exchanges gifts. The extended family of the celebrant helps to create a festive occasion.

Comments: This brief film is a good illustration of the fine detail in ordinary, middle-class Hindu ceremonialism. It is also a study of a rite not generally known, even to Indologists. A four-page user's guide is available on request.

Hindu Pilgrimage
   30 minutes, color, ¾" videocassette, 1975
   Sale $45.00
   David M. Knipe—Exploring the Religions of South Asia
   Department of South Asian Studies
   1242 Van Hise Hall
   University of Wisconsin—Madison
   Madison, WI 53706

This film treats the important Hindu practice of pilgrimage both as an outward journey and an inward experience. Professor Knipe names important, all-India pilgrimage sites (tirthas), as well as some sectarian centers and certain regional spots. He concludes his presentation by reminding his viewers that a pilgrimage is made not only to sacred places but also to objects such as trees or rocks. The bulk of the presentation focuses on activities in the town of Pandharper, Maharashtra, where pilgrims are shown congregating, joining processions, participating in group singing, and witnessing dramatic performances, after which they eventually "see" the image of Krishna in the form of Vithoba at the popular temple there. Shorter vignettes are also provided of other groups of pilgrims making ancestral offerings at the town of Gaya, and of pilgrims visiting shrines in and around the city of Kashi (Banaras), and elsewhere.

Comments: This is a helpful account of the subject; it is clear, coherent, and accessible to the independent learner. It includes careful attention to correct theoretical notions of pilgrimage.

Hindu Procession to the Sea
  8 minutes, color, 16mm, 1969
  Sale $100.00, Rental $6.00
  H. Daniel Smith—Image India
  Film Marketing Division/Film Rental Library
  Syracuse University
  1455 East Colvin Street
  Syracuse, NY 13210
  Also available from UCLA, WashSt, UWash

This film shows a procession in Madras City of a small group of urban devotees to the nearby sea for the annual (February or March) bath of an image of Lord Vishnu. After various religious and social activities in the procession, a small image substituted for the actual temple image is immersed in the surf. Worshippers plunge in the water at the same moment, the sins of a lifetime being removed by such a bath.

Comments: This is an excellent illustration of bhakti, and shows a wide diversity of devotees joyously participating in this festival bath. The film succeeds as an understatement, putting devotion in the realm of the everyday. It might be useful to contrast this film with a more awesome production like Yvonne Hanneman's *Murugan.*

The Hindu Ritual Sandhya
  19 minutes, color, 16mm, 1973
  Doris Srinivasan
  Inquire: Doris Srinivasan
  Department of Art History
  George Mason University
  Fairfax, VA 22030
  Also available from UCB, Purdue, NYU, UWisc

The film concentrates on an orthdox Smarta brahman in Maharashtra performing his sandhya, the personal ritual traditionally recognizing the junctures of day and night—dawn and twilight. The stages of sipping water, breath-control, application of ashes and sectarian marks, offering water, etc., lead up to the central recitation of the gayatri mantra and the recognition of the deities. The conclusion of the film claims to find the archaic origins of sandhya in man's uncertainty regarding solar rhythms and renewed contact with the sun.

Comments: The film is well produced, with good use of slides in cutaway sequences. The Sanskrit recitations of the ritualist underlie the constant narration—this lack of synchronized sound is slightly disconcerting. As there is somewhat more historical detail here than in the film by Professor Smith on the same subject (*Hindu Devotions at Dawn*), this film is perhaps better suited for advanced students. The two together provide a useful comparative study of the same ancient rite in two different regions, and both have accompanying guides.

The Hindu Sacrament of Surrender
   8 minutes, color, 16mm, 1969
   Sale $100.00, Rental $8.00
   H. Daniel Smith—Image India
   Film Marketing Division/Film Rental Library
   Syracuse University
   1455 East Colvin Street
   Syracuse, NY 13210
   Also available from UWash

Reenacted on film are the rites of initiation into a Sri-Vaishnava Tengalai sect in Madras, South India. Although both brahmans and nonbrahmans may be initiated, the principals here are a shudra husband and wife, both of whom go through five solemn purifying rites (pancasamskaras) under the direction of the family priest. The film presents in sequence branding of the initiates' shoulders with the sacred symbols of Vishnu, application of red and white "Y"-shaped marks to various parts of their bodies, the giving of a secret name and a special mantra, and the instruction in sacrifice or "surrender."

Comments: Professor Smith's film briefly portrays an important area of Hinduism seldom discussed and not previously photographed, namely the initiation of a believer into a sect or cult (rather than into a stage of life or monotheistic order). A brief glimpse of initiation with branding may be seen in Part Two of *Wedding of the Goddess*. The slow pace of the film lends credence to the solemnity of the ceremony. As the user's guide rightly cautions, this film is recommended for the advanced viewer who has a strong background in the general structures of Hindu ritual life.

Hindu Sacrament of Thread Investiture
   14 minutes, color, 16mm, 1969
   Sale $150.00, Rental $12.00
   H. Daniel Smith—Image India
   Film Marketing Division/Film Rental Library
   Syracuse University
   1455 East Colvin Street
   Syracuse, NY 13210
   Also available from UIowa, OklaSt, UWash

Professor Smith's film of the upanayana in a Sri-Vaishnava Tengalai community in Madras, South India, captures the life-cycle rite of investiture with the sacred thread, or initiation and "second birth" of a brahman boy. A ritual bath, fire offerings, symbolic and actual tonsure, investiture with thread, garments and staff, and the many stages of religious instruction are emphasized as the boy achieves his twice-born status in the Hindu community.

Comments: This is an excellent study of what still remains from Vedic religion as one of the most significant rites of Hinduism. Through careful and sensitive cinematography and narration the details are presented as a concrete whole. A six-page user's guide is available on request. Professor Knipe's *The Life Cycle in Hinduism: Birth, Initiation, Marriage* provides a comparison with its attention to the same ritual in North India.

Hindu Sacraments of Childhood: The First Five Years
    25 minutes, color, 16mm, 1969
    Sale $100.00, Rental $12.00
    H. Daniel Smith—Image India
    Film Marketing Division/Film Rental Library
    Syracuse University
    1455 East Colvin Street
    Syracuse, NY 13210
    Also available from ArizSt, UIowa, WashSt, UWash, UWisc

This film covers several samskaras, the important life-cycle or transition rites during the first five years of childhood. Following two prenatal rites intended to secure a son and assure his safe delivery, a Tengalai Sri-Vaishnava brahman boy, in the company of his family and the family priest, undergoes the birth ceremony, the name-giving ceremony, the rite at the first feeding with solid food, and the ritual tonsure that marks the commencement of the boy's education.

Comments: This is an excellent presentation of six of the samskaras surviving in contemporary Hinduism from Vedic religion. The cinematography and narration are clear and balanced, and a wealth of detail is vividly projected. A user's guide is available on request. For comparison and contrast with these South Indian rituals, the same rites performed in North India may be seen in Professor Knipe's *The Life Cycle in Hinduism: Birth, Initiation, Marriage.*

Hindu Temple Rites: Bathing the Image of God
    13 minutes, color, 16mm, 1969
    Sale $140.00, Rental $12.00
    H. Daniel Smith—Image India

Film Marketing Division/Film Rental Library
Syracuse University
1455 East Colvin Street
Syracuse, NY 13210
Also available from UCLA, UIowa, WashSt, UWash, UWisc

This film portrays an annual festival, performed early in March in a small Sri-Vaishnava Tengalai village temple thirty miles from Madras. The images of Vishnu and his consorts Shri and Bhu are given summer libations of mantras, curds, milk, honey, coconut water, and powder. The dressing of the deities is shown, as is the offering of prasada, food given to the gods and returned as consecrated to the handful of villagers present. The special worship, a shower bath for the gods, is inserted into the normative puja routine.

Comments: This is an effective presentation of the common pattern of puja, heightened by the insertion of a particular, occasional, or special ceremony. It details graphically the color, drama, and dignity of temple worship. In conjunction with the viewing of the film, it would be helpful for the student to read general materials on the structure of ordinary and extraordinary Hindu puja and to have some knowledge of the history and iconography of Vishnu.

The Hindu World
10 minutes, color, 16mm, 1963
Sale $150.00
Robert M. Perry
Coronet Instructional Films
65 East South Water Street
Chicago, IL 60601
Also available from ArizSt, UCt, FlaSt, Boise, NoIll, UIll, IndU, UMe, BU, UMich, UMinn, SyrU, KentSt, USoCar, BYU, UWisc

Utilizing views of ancient temples, shots of statues, and scenes of Hindu religious rites, this film undertakes a brief survey of the historical and cultural factors contributing to the development of Hinduism. It mentions the caste system, the belief in reincarnation, and the fact that religion exerts an influence on the Hindu way of life. Some attention is also given to the "yogas" which provide mental and physical discipline, and which have left their indelible traces on Hindu civilization.

Comments: The above description of this film's contents is not unlike what is found in most film catalogues at the many rental libraries listing the title. It makes the film seem much more attractive and relevant as a resource for learning about Hinduism than it is. A critical consideration of the statement may raise some questions about the pedagogical trade-offs in the utilization of an eleven-minute film covering the "Hindu World." Temple architecture, the social and religious significance of temple institutions, India's heritage of religious art, the meaning and techniques of ritual behavior, the intricacies of over 3,000 years of history, the milieu of the social and cultural complex in which Hinduism as a religion has continued to thrive—to what degree can any one, let alone all, of these factors be identified, examined, and illuminated in the span of eleven minutes? As for the dynamics of caste in village and urban settings, in classical or contemporary times—what kinds of analyses or even examples does such a brief, panoramic treatment permit? The same must be asked in regard to the many ideological structures and belief systems, here merely mentioned in passing. The trade-off for the convenience of brevity or modest rental fee of such a production as this is to settle for intolerable generalizations and imprecise oversimplifications. The result is to present not the "Hindu world" but a fantasy creation, at best a name-dropping essay. This film, despite its popularity at secondary school levels, cannot be recommended for college-level learning programs whether of independent or classroom structure. Using such a production as this is clearly counterproductive. It can only generate facile disregard for the complexities of a culture, and only perpetuate a lamentably superficial approach to the study of the social and spiritual dimensions of the Hindu way of life. The evaluation committee feels there are preferable alternatives now readily available in film for use during the introductory phases of the study of Hindu religion and Indian culture (see the Topical Index).

Hinduism
   18 minutes, b/w, 16mm, 1962
   Sale $145.00, Rental $20.00
   The Great Religions Series
   National Film Board of Canada
   1251 Avenue of the Americas
   New York, NY 10020
   Also available from ArizSt, UCB, FlaSt, NoIll, UIll, Purdue, IowaSt, UIowa, BU, UNeb, SyrU, KentSt, PennSt, BYU

This film presents the so-called "three ways" of Hinduism (jnana, karma, and bhakti), and a fourth section on "modern Hinduism."

Comments: Although this was once the most widely used film for general survey courses, it is now dated and cannot be recommended. For more adequate introductions to Hindu religion and Indian culture, see the Topical Index.

Hinduism and the Song of God
  30 minutes, color, 16mm, 1975
  Sale $325.00, Rental $35.00
  Elda Hartley—Films for a New Age series
  Hartley Productions, Inc.
  Cat Rock Road
  Cos Cob, CT 06807

This colorful film opens with a miscellany of shots taken at various sites throughout the subcontinent, presenting "India" impressionistically to the uninitiated viewer. There follows a central expository section based on a *Gita*-derived concept that those who adhere to Hinduism belong to one of three groups, or "yogas"—jnana, karma, or the "most popular" bhakti. Each is identified at some length in the narration to the accompaniment of striking, and sometimes illuminating, pictorial sequences (e.g., depiction of a Hatha Yoga adept, footage of pilgrimage activities, a scene showing tulasi worship). Also, the four "life stages" are briefly recounted. A closing section attempts to convey something of the dynamics of contemporary Hinduism by presenting sequences of the widely popular charismatic, Sathya Sai Baba (b. 1926), with impressive crowd scenes to suggest his influence.

Comments: This film divided the evaluation panel between those who, on the one hand, regarded it as an adequate—if glossy—general survey of Hindu ideals, and those who, on the other hand, judged it to be so superficial and generalizing that its effect is to be seriously misleading and dangerously distorting. All agreed, however, that this prize-winning and widely advertised film is, indeed, visually appealing, and that it would invariably be received warmly by viewers unfamiliar with things Hindu and Indian. The point of view which prevailed among the panelists was that the picture of India and of Hinduism presented in this film is, simply, *too* pretty: all is sweetness and light, sunshine on blue waters, fresh flowers with best saris, polished brass, and improbable smiles—all front and center for the camera. Even the man reclining on a bed of nails is smiling. Moreover, most of the people depicted are obviously drawn from urbanite, upper classes. Because so many complexities, contradictions, and details have been omitted in this neatly packaged presentation, and because at least an acknowledgement of such matters is essential for an adequate understanding of the Hindu religious tradition, the panel as a whole felt unable to recommend this film either for independent learning purposes or for classroom utilization.

For those who feel compelled to seek out a film, which within thirty minutes' screen time attempts to deal with Hinduism as a whole, attention is drawn to a more recent production from the same source, *India and the Infinite: The Soul of a People* (q.v.). This film essay addresses the problem of the variety within the great Hindu tradition.

Other panoramic introductions to Indian civilization and Hindu culture can also be found in *Hinduism: Many Paths to God* and in *Hinduism: 330 Million Gods*, both reviewed elsewhere in this section. The panel suggests, however, that because in recent years so many responsible films on more specialized aspects of Hinduism have appeared, it is no longer necessary to be satisfied with the built-in inadequacies of panoramic surveys, or with highly dubious and often misleading interpretations endemic to generic treatments. (See the Topical Index for titles leading to available resources on specific aspects of Hinduism.)

Hinduism in South India
    30 minutes, color, ¾″ videocassette, 1975
    Sale $45.00
    David M. Knipe—Exploring the Religions of South Asia
    Department of South Asian Studies
    1242 Van Hise Hall
    University of Wisconsin—Madison
    Madison, WI 53706

This presentation throws its focus on the "distinct civilization" of South India. According to the guest lecturer, Professor George V. Hart III, the predominant religion in the area of the Deccan ("South India") is an amalgam of imported northern, Vedic religious forms and ideas with ancient southern, Dravidian notions and practices. The first half of the program consists of the recommendation of certain theoretical frameworks within which to view the great diversity of South Indian phenomena: those which recognize the incorporation of agricultural motifs into a world view; those which uphold social stratification into caste according to pollution ideologies; those which perceive women as personifications of power, both benign (or "ordered") and threatening (or "disordered"); and those which maintain in certain forms of temple worship the symbolism of royal presence and celebrations. The last half of the program consists of a ceremony in which a Telugu-speaking brahman (Professor V. Narayana Rao) directs a young man who performs worship to the elephant-headed deity Ganesa or Ganapati, and a brief resume of a story told among Shaivites of the famous saint Siruttondar, one of the sixty-three Nayanmars.

Comments: This videocassette provides an understanding of North-South regional differences in India, and also, in a segment of a rite in Telugu and Sanskrit, the interaction of the Sanskritic with the vernacular traditions. The segment of the Ganapati ritual excerpted gives a good sense of pace for Hindu rituals. The focus on the Nayanmar saintly tradition is unique in film resources.

Hinduism: Many Paths to God
   29 minutes, color, 16mm, 1973
   Sale $415.00, Rental $28.00
   Howard Enders; ABC TV
   Xerox Films
   245 Long Hill Road
   Middletown, CT 06457
   Also available from UIll, UMinn, UWash

This film includes: Baba, a holy man (or sannyasin) of northern India; extensive footage of the Ganges from the foot of the Himalayas, past Rishikesh and Hardwar to Banaras; and vast crowds at the Ardha Kumbha Mela, a major festival at Hardwar. It presents an interview with an Indian historian, Professor Romila Thapar, concerning polytheism/monotheism, and explores Western questions concerning the Ganges, e.g., its pollution, holiness, power. This film provides a substantial presentation of the festival of Durga with excellent footage of Durga devotees, a holy man at Vrindavana walking in the footsteps of Krishna, and closes with scenes of Banaras and the Ganges and a passage from the *Bhagavad Gita*.

Comments: This film, made expressly for television, shows the positive effects of a substantial budget, expert crew, and adept narration. The emphasis on meditation and reflection contributes to the general appeal of the film but should not be considered to be a comprehensive presentation of Hinduism. Though relatively successful as a general introduction to Hinduism, this film illustrates the overall limitation of a brief panoramic treatment; for more specific aspects of Hinduism, see the Topical Index. It is appropriate for beginning students and enjoyable viewing on any level.

Hinduism: Part I
Hinduism: Part II
Hinduism: Part III
   90 minutes, b/w, 16mm, 1955, 1962
   Sale discontinued, Rental $9.50
   Huston Smith; NET—The Religions of Man
   Audio-Visual Center
   Indiana University
   Bloomington, IN 47401
   Also available from ArizSt, UCB, IncU, KentSt

These are three half-hour cinescopes (16mm, b/w films made of a televised presentation), addressed to Hinduism as a system of religious thought. They are themselves part of a larger series called The Religions of Man. The series, written by and featuring Huston Smith, later became a book by the same name, and that book has been for over two decades one of the most widely used popular surveys of the world's religions in the English-speaking world. The television series—of which these three illustrated lectures formed a part—was famous in no small degree due to the winsome charm and disarming enthusiasm of the well-informed Professor Smith. The cinescope film versions of the program were for many years staples in film rental libraries and television archives, and they assisted those who saw them to approach religious traditions other than their own with sensitivity to important ideological issues and awareness of basic human values.

Comments: These programs—at least the three on Hinduism—have long since been superseded not only by more recent, target treatments of selected Hindu phenomena and the specialized foci these imply, but also by modern techniques of production technology which make these early efforts seem dated by comparison. There are many copies of these programs still in circulation throughout the country and these prints are evidently still used by community groups and in secondary schools for the study of Hinduism. While the distributors may justly be proud of Huston Smith's series for the positive contributions which it made to the public's sensitivity to the religions of the world, the films should be gracefully withdrawn from circulation. They have served their pedagogical purpose admirably, but to serious students of the religions of man they are now largely of historical interest only. For reference to recommended films see the Topical Index under such specific entries as: Worship, Symbol, Samskara, Ritual, Pilgrimage.

Hinduism: 330 Million Gods
   54 minutes, color, 16mm, 1977
   Sale $750.00, Rental $100.00
   (Also available in videocassette)
   Peter Montagnon for BBC-TV—The Long Search series
   Time-Life Multimedia
   P.O. Box 644 100 Eisenhower Drive
   Paramus, NJ 07652

Narrator-host Ronald Eyre candidly admits during the early minutes of this film's introduction to Hinduism that there is great difficulty in knowing who to trust in the long search for understanding the nature of religion. "Scholarly people talk history; devout people push their own brand of devotion; busy people haven't the time to talk to you; simple people don't have the words for it; the holiest people keep their mouths shut." After a series of sequences along the Ganges at Banaras, Allahabad, and Hardwar to illustrate a Hindu penchant for bathing, for mass festivals, and for pilgrimage, he settles into a village in north Bihar for the remainder of the film. In this microcosmic setting, the viewer is shown several passing sights suggestive of pan-

Indian daily life and social concerns. Some attention is given to the four main "castes" ("an institutionalization of the division of labor"), and to the four stages of life. As part of the treatment of the latter, the rituals which mark entry into the first two stages of life are depicted by showing scenes from village celebrations of a mass thread investiture and of a wedding. The camera gives somewhat more focused attention to what are presumably representative aspects of Hindu piety encountered in the village: two separate celebrations of Saraswati-puja; a "sannyas" figure who is "beyond the gods"; a fire ritual performed to insure a good harvest; some brahmans at their morning prayers; and liturgies performed in a temple dedicated to Shiva. What seems to exercise the curiosity of Eyre most of all, a theme to which he returns on more than one occasion, is the "problem" of the many gods of Hindu piety in relation to the existence of the "real god," Brahman. The many sects of believers, the different places ascribed with holy presence and power, the various activities demonstrating devotion, the multiplicity of deities—all these cause Eyre to ruminate upon what in fact unites Hindus. He closes his presentation by implying that it may be the search itself which unites them spiritually: ". . . their will to come closer to God by whatever means best suits them—worship and devotion to the ordinary man, knowledge and the mind for those with the gift for it—no way excluded, no way preferred so long as the destination gets nearer all the time."

Comments: This was the first of the widely disseminated "Long Search" programs that BBC filmed on location for later TV broadcast. Fortunately for the series, the programs improved later on (see the companion volume, *Focus on Buddhism*, for reviews of *Buddhism: Footprint of the Buddha—India* and of *Buddhism: Land of the Disappearing Buddha—Japan*). Its early position in the series also explains Eyre's preamble about preparing for the long search, an otherwise perplexing statements near the beginning of the film. BBC and Eyre had evidently planned a second film to focus on the spiritual teachings of Hinduism, but the project had to be abandoned due to Government of India prohibition against further BBC filming in India at the time. As a result, the single program available presents a somewhat spotty, off-balance, and incomplete picture of the Hindu religious tradition .

The decision to confine most of the footage to a North Indian village is both a strength and a weakness in the production. On the one hand, by showing several times the village temple and its bathing ghat, the foreign appears familiar. On the other hand, the potential of the village setting has not been adequately exploited; this fault is due in no small measure to the choice of the particular English-speaking informant, a professor of philosophy who had emigrated to Surrey, England, and has returned to his native village for the occasion of the filming. He is utilized at length unproductively; however attractive and likable he seems, he simply does not come across forcefully enough as a personality, nor is he allowed to move the discussion beyond Eyre's rather naive level of questioning. What emerges from their combination is a bland dialogue leading to conventional conclusions about Hinduism's inclusiveness, punctuated by Eyre's own recurring questions about the many gods. (Actually, only a very few deities are mentioned by name: Ganesha, Kali, Lakshmi, Saraswati, Brahma, Vishnu, Shiva, and the unexplained concept of a "powerhouse" consort, or shakti.) The visuals are well photographed, occasionally splendid; the narration is engaging, occasionally eloquent. The sum of the parts is, however, less than it should be. Despite its honorable intentions, the film will probably produce low yields in an academic setting. While it bears a second viewing, it is unlikely that college-level audiences will be motivated to do so. No study guide comes with rental copies of the film, but attention is called to the availability of *A Student's Guide to the Long Search* (Miami-Dade College) for those who subscribe to the entire Long Search series course package, and to Dr. Ninian Smart's introductory survey, *The Long Search* (New York: Little Brown). However, neither provides guidance for what one sees in the film nor to the issues taken up in the narration. For another, shorter filmic essay on the "problem" which so frustrated and finally eluded Eyre, see *India and the Infinite*. . . . For more specific aspects of Hinduism treated in films, see the Topical Index, below.

Hinduism: Wheel of Karma
   21 minutes, color, 16mm, 1968
   Sale $315.00, Rental $29.00
   Lew Ayres—Altars of the World
   Threshold Films
   2025 North Highland Avenue
   Hollywood, CA 90068

This film is an attempt to summarize the religious praxis of Hinduism, but makes no inroads into its social context. It includes many stock scenes—wedding, cremation, yoga adept in action, temple worship, street scenes, and temple shots—against a background describing Hindu religious practices as an attempt to escape the cycle of births and rebirths. It also discusses mantra and prana yoga as methods.

Comments: This film is simplistic and patronizing—" . . .Water, mountains, trees, stones, animals, yes even the cow, are treated as 'holy'"—and it fails to make valid distinctions *within* Hinduism regionally, communally, historically, etc., in favor of stressing the "tolerance" and "variety" within "the one Hinduism." The mispronunciation of several words representing central concepts within Hinduism is only one of the clues revealing that little expert help was sought or gained in the production or planning of this film. This film, like the others in the series (once more revived by its latest distributor, and yet again assigned a recent release date), attempts to prove that Hinduism, like all the great religions of the world, is founded on the golden rule.

Holy Men of India: The Sadhus
10 minutes, color, 16mm, 1968, discontinued
Lew Ayres (Doubleday Multimedia)
(Although discontinued by the distributor, this film is still available through numerous, regional film rental libraries)
Also available from ArizSt

Hardwar, city of holy men of various sects, is the setting for most of the scenes in this film—scenes of religious specialists engaged in individual study, yogic exercises, worshiping alone or in groups at an ashram. Particularly memorable are close-ups of a number of faces, and the sequence devoted to the bodily contortions of a practitioner of Hatha Yoga.

Comments: This film is essentially a series of disconnected shots held together only thinly by a narrative line. It is not a useful film—nullified by its general "Barnum & Bailey" approach to Hindu mysticism and its often misleading narrative. However, used imaginatively and under the proper circumstances, it could become an effective pedagogical tool. For example, in the study of Yoga, one could use this film without sound, excerpting its footage of the Hatha Yogin doing his contortions. Or one could show it, accompanied by one's own commentary, simply to give an insight into the value placed upon "the holy man" and his extraordinary lifestyle in India. But potential users are advised that other, more responsible treatments of these topics are available (see the Topical Index).

How a Hindu Worships: At the Home Shrine
18 minutes, color, 16mm, 1969
Sale $190.00, Rental $15.00
H. Daniel Smith—Image India
Film Marketing Division/Film Rental Library
Syracuse University
1455 East Colvin Street
Syracuse, NY 13210

This film is perhaps the most important of the eleven in Professor Smith's Image India series. In focusing upon domestic worship, it portrays one of the most significant, yet one of the least known dimensions of Hinduism. Filmed in the city of Madras in a Sri-

Vaishnava Tengalai brahman household, a middle-class office worker, assisted by his wife, performs his daily early morning worship of the image of Krishna in the home shrine. This griharchana is detailed and explained in all its complexity, step-by-step, the narration blending with descriptive comments on the underlying mythical and philosophical basis for the puja. Specific attention is given to the vyuha doctrine of the Vaishnavas, the belief in the five modes of being of Vishnu, the image itself, and the arca mode of the deity being represented in the film as the object of worship.

Comments: This is a first-rate presentation of the structure of household worship, and one suitable for undergraduate, graduate, and general audiences in the classroom or in independent learning situations. The accompanying guide (available on request), with a plan of the shrine itself, is helpful in following the procedures of the ritual. This film is an excellent supplement to cinematographic treatment of temple worship, and demonstrates the great importance of household shrines in the religious life of many Hindus.

India and the Infinite: The Soul of A People
   27 minutes, color, 16mm, 1979
   Sale $350.00, Rental $40.00
   Elda Hartley—Films for a New Age series
   Narrator: Huston Smith
   Hartley Productions, Inc.
   Cat Rock Road
   Cos Cob, Ct 06807

This film strikes a characteristic note early on; its emphasis is on diversity. "India seems to include everything," observes narrator Huston Smith, and as he talks the camera supplements his inventory of the different racial types, the several languages, the variety of lifestyles, the many legitimate goals, the widely contrasting values, the countless deities, the numerous religions found in the subcontinent by bringing to the screen striking visual clips to emphasize the spoken word. "What a bewildering chaos, what a jungle of life and thought" India presents; it "swarms with life and vitality. Nothing seems to have been overlooked, nothing excluded." In a further development of his thoughts, Smith moves on, musing ". . . if the visible India excludes nothing, that in the invisible which excludes nothing is the Infinite. The soul of India is the Infinite." What for Smith is a statement about a culture is also to his way of thinking an accurate description of the individual within that culture: in each person, regardless of social status, age, or degree of sophistication, there is a divinity, an "infinite dimension" of being to be cultivated. And in India, Smith suggests, the way the culture has manifested its soul most authentically, just as the way the individual within that culture has learned to recognize an affinity with the Infinite, is through the arts.

There follows an extended digression, then, on the arts in India. The purpose of the arts in India, states Smith in this later section of the film, is "to *in*form and *trans*form—inform us of the way things truly *are*, transform us into what we might truly *be*." In particular, he submits, sculpture "tokens timelessness and eternity. The Indians saw no point in carving replicas. . . . Art's opportunity is to see deeper than we usually do, to see the Infinite stirring in things. . . . We must receive [the shapes depicted in great Hindu religious sculpture] as images of what we ourselves are potentially." Throughout this digression the screen is transformed by more or less fleeting pictures of cast bronzes and sculpted stones, of dancers in action and in momentary repose, of storied temples and sunlit spires. The film ends by returning to the metaphor used at the beginning of the film, reminding the traveler who wishes to undertake the journey to India that her "soil lies as close as your travel agent." As for her soul, we are told that "here is a place one cannot reach by going anywhere."

Comments: This film attempts to achieve two goals simultaneously: it presents at once a cornucopia of scenes from across the length and breadth of India collected over the years by filmmaker Elda Hartley. It is as well an eloquent, spoken reflection on the soil and the soul of India by Huston Smith. Hence, it is both a statement rich in visual content and also an essay on man's religious quest. Both efforts succeed admirably. The film is a pleasure for the eye to see, the ear to hear. This is not the first venture together by this filmmaker and philosopher— they collaborated earlier on *Requiem for a Faith* (on Tibetan Bud-dhism) and on *Islamic Mysticism: The Sufi Way*—but this is the most successful teaming to date. With this film, they complete a trilogy on three of the world's great religions. Still, not everything is right about this film by any means: the ending does not really work; the dance sequences used as a transition from the Nataraja icon are unfortunate examples of the tradition; and not all may find Professor Smith's synthesis of the four varnas, life-stages, yogas, and personality types convincing. Nonetheless the film fills a need to address directly the phenomenon of Hindu India's diversity (see reviews of *Hinduism and the Song of God* and *Hinduism: 330 Million Gods* elsewhere in this section). Presented as a film in the genre of an audio/visual essay, it may provide for many beginning students a vivid and compelling introduction to material about which they might wish to learn more. The imaginative instructor will find ways to juxtapose this film with other panoramic treatments of Hinduism, or preferably with other monographic films on specific aspects of Hinduism (for which see Topical Index).

Indian Holy Men: Darshan
  28 minutes, color, 16mm, 1972
  Sale $225.00, Rental $35.00
  Satyam Shivam Sundaram and Florence Davey
  New Line Cinema Corporation
  853 Broadway, 16th Floor
  New York, NY 10003

The film begins with a series of unexplained views of men who are presumably holy. There are only a few sentences of narration in this part, summarily contending that in India "each follows a discipline suited to his nature." Then come quick sketches of four particular men reputed in India to be holy. The first man portrayed is the head of a Radha-Krishna sect in Vrndavan. He is shown ritually bathing in the early morning, attended by his disciples to whom he gives a lecture in Hindi on Brahmananda (the highest bliss), and detachedly seated in a courtyard feeding the pigeons and parrots swirling about him. The second holy man is a shakta who, although deaf and mute, is divinely happy in his worship and dance to the goddess in his Himalayan shrine. The third holy man is a recluse who lives in a cave (not shown) on the upper Ganges, and the last maintains a Shiva temple made holy by his deceased guru.

Comments: Except for the opening scenes, this film is acceptably filmed and narrated. It makes no attempt to show what the populace thinks of these men, except by indicating that they do have their followers and reputations in society at large. The film is uncritical of these men and their pursuits, and does not attempt to give any detailed information about their ritual or beliefs. There is no guide with the film. For these reasons the film *Four Holy Men* . . . seems preferable for educational use; yet this film is certainly suitable as a supplement to it.

An Indian Pilgrimage: Kashi
  30 minutes, color, 16mm, 1969
  Sale $135.00, Rental $17.00
  Michael Camerini and Mira Reym Binford
  Department of South Asian Studies
  1242 Van Hise Hall
  University of Wisconsin—Madison
  Madison, WI 53706
  Also available from WashSt, UWash

This film gives an overview of a typical pilgrimage to India's holiest city. It shows two middle-aged, middle-class couples enroute to various holy places in Kashi, performing sacred rituals such as offerings for ancestors, and puja on the Ganges. These four pilgrims are given elaborate instructions by a priest on how to conduct the various rituals and how to make their pilgrimage most efficacious. The film shows pilgrimage as a social as well as religious experience.

Comments: This is a visually rich, varied, and entirely authentic presentation: it is particularly helpful in showing the blend of the ideal ritual form with a touch of pragmatic sham in religious practices (e.g., one priest's clever schemes to raise the honorarium for his prayers for the pilgrims' ancestors). This film is ideal for any course in Hinduism, and particularly useful in a part of a course treating pilgrimmage, holy places, and religious practices. Only general knowledge is required to benefit from this film; it will probably generate considerable discussion. It is highly regarded due to its clarity of conception and excellent narration. See also *An Indian Pilgrimage: Ramdevra* in the same series, below.

An Indian Pilgrimage: Ramdevra
   26 minutes, color, 16mm, 1974
   Sale $125.00, Rental $17.00
   Michael Camerini and Mira Reym Binford
   Department of South Asian Studies
   1242 Van Hise Hall
   University of Wisconsin—Madison
   Madison, WI 53706
   Also available from ArizSt, UKans, UUtah, WashSt, UWash

This film traces a group of pilgrims who travel from Bombay to Ramdevra's grave in Rajasthan. Speaking in Hindi (with English subtitles), the pilgrims reveal a wide range of motives for the pilgrimage, including family, health, business, and thanksgiving. At the pilgrimage site—the grave of the fifteenth-century Rajasthani saint-hero Ramdevra—the pilgrims present their symbolic offering (a small silver statue of a horse, representing Ramdevra's martial powers), and receive prasad (food blessed by the god). The pilgrims also participate in a mela, a large fair annually held near the pilgrimage site, thus showing the easy blend of sacred and secular in the typical Indian pilgrimage. The film also explains the significance of Ramdevra in the interplay of Hindu and Muslim elements in many Indian cults; it also demonstrates the role of bhajans (devotional songs) in sustaining and spreading a cult such as Ramdevra's.

Comments: This film succeeds admirably on many counts: in addition to being a completely authentic presentation of a pilgrimage, it sheds considerable light on religious practice, bhakti, religious symbolism, Hindu-Muslim relations, and devotional music. It shows a remarkable sequence of a woman in an ecstatic trance as well as several sequences which candidly reveal the pilgrims in devotional singing and enjoying religious and secular delights of the pilgrimage sites.

The Indians and the Sacred
  50 minutes, color, 16mm, 1972
  Sale $795.00, Rental $75.00
  Louis Malle—Phantom India
  New Yorker Films
  16 West 61st Street
  New York, NY 10023

Although all of the seven films in Louis Malle's series include brief treatments of Indian religion, this is the only one which has religion as its primary concern. The film shows a devotee of Murugan, the temple complex at Madurai, local priests, holy men and beggars, as well as the faithful performing puja and various rituals. Malle frequently lets the camera rest on a quiet Indian street scene or an immobile face while he expounds his theories, suppositions, and unabashed confusion concerning the varieties of Hindu theory and practice.

Comments: The opening sequence of this film, which shows an ecstatic devotee of Murugan with numerous spears piercing his flesh, well reveals Malle's attempt to emphasize, without explaining, the sensational and apparently negative aspects of the Hindu religious tradition. Consistent with Malle's thesis, this film treats religion as both the cause of and the way of escape from the poverty and misery of Indian life. Malle frequently refers to devotees as fanatical, and to Hinduism as pessimistic, and he provides no context by which to render intelligible the seemingly bizarre and destructive behavior of the devout Hindus shown in this visually rich but uninformed film. Potential users of this film may find it informative to read the reviews of Malle's other films in this series—*Calcutta, A Look at the Castes, On the Fringes of Indian Society,* and *Things Seen in Madras*—all of which will be found in Part Two of this volume. His predominantly negative attitude toward Hinduism represents a striking contrast to the effusive enthusiasm which informs so many other filmmakers' productions.

An Introduction: Exploring the Religions of South Asia
  30 minutes, color, ¾″ videocassette, 1975
  Sale $45.00
  David M. Knipe—Exploring the Religions of South Asia
  Department of South Asian Studies
  1242 Van Hise Hall
  University of Wisconsin—Madison
  Madison, WI 53706

This film serves as an introduction not only to the series Exploring the Religions of South Asia, but to the geography and races, languages and cultures, sights and sounds, people and activities, and a host of other factors to be kept in mind by anyone who would seriously undertake a study of religions in South Asia. Focusing on India, Professor Knipe suggests that there are four "widely shared" concepts, or configurations, to remember when studying the "montage" of religions there: (1) the enduring folk traditions, or "popular" grass-roots religions; that is, practices which persist just beneath the surface of the literary "establishment" doctrines of the Great Religions; (2) the pervasive concept of samsara; (3) the religious basis for society found in such classical Indian expressions as varnasramadharma, and perpetuated in the communal divisions of Hindu society known as jati, or "the caste system"; and (4) an understanding of the religious basis of the individual as "in process" throughout life stages toward a transcendent ideal of perfection. These ordering principals apply, perhaps unevenly, to the five religious traditions presented in this series: Hinduism, Buddhism, Jainism, Islam, and Christianity.

Comments: The latter part of this introductory program previews how the other videotapes in the series will contribute to the difficult and far-reaching job of surveying the religions of South Asia; it is perhaps relevant primarily to the needs of those who will utilize those other tapes. And, for users who do complete the entire "course" of tape presentations, a later reviewing of this section of the introductory program is highly recommended.

Kundalini Yoga
  57 minutes, color, ¾" videocassette, 1976
  Sale $275.00
  Lynn Madlener and Joseph Campbell—Psyche & Symbol
  Teletape Associates
  2728 Durant Avenue
  Berkeley, CA 94704

This is one of a series of videotapes of Professor Joseph Campbell lecturing with slides on myths and symbols in Homer, Dante, the Tibetan Book of the Dead, the traditions of the Navaho Indians, and from a contemporary woman undergoing psychoanalysis. C. G. Jung's *Man and His Symbols* and Campbell's *The Mythic Image* provide the bibliographic core of the course. Part Two of the series, "The Visionary Journey," is concerned with the psychological journey of the self, upward in kundalini yoga, downward in the Tibetan Book of the Dead, and both directions in Dante. While the series is meant to be taken as a course, Program six alone includes concentrated discussions of Hindu phenomena. Yoga, the seven chakras, the sri-yantra, Shiva, the goddess, and so forth, are illustrated and presented in this program.

Comments: Professor Campbell is a convincing lecturer. The discussion of the chakras, which takes up the bulk of the program, is sustained and substantial for an undergraduate or independent learning situation, and includes the Sanskrit terminology. Professor Campbell knows the material well and presents comparative illustrations that encourage the viewer to consider broader contents, although many may dispute the "universality" claimed for the South Asian symbols under discussion. Unfortunately, the production is limited technically to that of a taped lecture, confined to the lecturer, his back to the camera half the time, pointing to static slides on a screen. This 1976 production does not once use contemporary video techniques to alleviate the lecture format, and a viewer accustomed to variation and mobility feels trapped in a simulated lecture-hall audience. Professor Wendy Doniger O'Flaherty has prepared an excellent study guide which should be read in advance.

The Life Cycle in Hinduism: Birth, Initiation, Marriage
  30 minutes, color, ¾″ videocassette, 1974
  Sale $45.00
  David M. Knipe—Exploring the Religions of South Asia
  Department of South Asian Studies
  1242 Van Hise Hall
  University of Wisconsin—Madison
  Madison, WI 53706

This program focuses on the rites which mark events associated with birth, initiation, and marriage among orthoprax, brahmanically-oriented Hindus. Knipe's subjects are North Indians drawn largely from the middle and well-to-do classes. The subtitles in this program are especially helpful as precise identifications for the "transition rites" depicted: anaprashana, or "first feeding"; chudakarana, or "ritual tonsure"; upanayana, or "initiation"; and vivaha, or "marriage"—all of which samskaras are shown. Two central points of this program are (1) these ancient brahmanical rites of passage are still performed attentively by families throughout India, and (2) one finds homogeneity in their celebration whether observed in the North or the South of India, whether done by rich or poor, or whether performed among educated or uneducated Hindus.

Comments: The visuals are memorable and Knipe's narration is intelligent and clear, making this brief treatment a forceful resource for the independent learner or for the classroom student. It is particularly relevant for an implicit demonstration of Hinduism's enduring commitment to the pattern of a dispersed domestic cult centering in the home rather than to a congregational form of worship primarily dependent upon attendance at temple celebrations. While some viewers may find the tonsure rite performed on a three-year-old girl extraordinary and the marriage ceremony of two twelve-year-olds irregular, Knipe endeavors to put these into a larger contextual framework. Viewers interested in other films on these and other rites of passage, or transition, may consult the Topical Index under Samskara, Children, Education, Initiation, Marriage, Rituals, etc. It should be noted that this videocassette was designed to be used in combination with *Death and Rebirth in Hinduism,* #15 in the series Exploring the Religions of South Asia.

Living Hinduism
  30 minutes, color, ¾″ videocassette, 1975
  Sale $45.00
  David M. Knipe—Exploring the Religions of South Asia
  Department of South Asian Studies
  1242 Van Hise Hall
  University of Wisconsin—Madison
  Madison, WI 53706

This film suggests that in order to understand the "incorrigible inclusiveness" of Hinduism it is helpful to recognize, on the one hand, the "ground structure" (little traditions) of Hindu folk religion, and on the other hand, the "superstructure" (great tradition) of the pan-Indian, literary, and doctrinal teachings of establishment Hinduism. The film emphasizes popular elements such as celebrating the presence of powers in trees, stones, water, fields, planets, animals and serpents. The film treats Hindu religious specialists—shamans, musicians, priests, pandits, mahants, and yogis. Attention is given to t¹ e place of women in living Hinduism, to the importance of sectarian Hinduism, and to tantrism. These are elaborated upon later in the series, most notably in films #3, #4, and #5.

Comments: This program is particularly useful for the introduction it affords to basic categories and terminologies which are encountered in most advanced treatments of Hindu religious and social life. The setting given them here is intelligently simplified. The chosen approach to the phenomenon of diversity in Hinduism provides instructive contrast to that utilized in *India and the Infinite* . . .(q.v.).

Major Religions of the World
  20 minutes, color, 16mm, 1954
  Sale $290.00
  (b/w version—Sale $175.00; Rental 1-3 days, $21.00)
  Encyclopedia Britannica Educational Corp.
  425 North Michigan Avenue
  Chicago, IL 60611

Also available from ArizSt, UAriz, UCol, UCt, FlaSt, USoFla, NoIll, SoIll, UIll, IndSt, IndU, IowaSt, UIowa, UKans, UMe, BU, UMich, UMinn, UMo, UNeb, SyrU, UNoCar, KentSt, OklaSt, PennSt, USoCar, UTenn, BYU, UUtah, WashSt, UWash, UWisc

This broad-spectrum survey looks briefly at Hinduism, moves quickly on to view Buddhism as a world religion, then shifts to the origin, spread, and present strength of Islam before attention turns to the two religions given most attention, namely Judaism and Christianity. In the treatment of Christianity, equal treatment is given to Roman Catholic, Greek Catholic, and Protestant branches of Christianity. Scriptures, general ideologies, and crucial rituals are stressed in varying degrees for each religion surveyed.

Comments: One distributor's rental records show that this film is still used, notably in public high schools and church groups. This is unfortunate: to compress five of the complex religions of the world into twenty minutes necessitates oversimplification and superficiality. Because of the greater emphasis given to Judaism and the three major forms of Christianity, only two or three minutes are devoted to Hinduism—clearly insufficient for this massively complex religious culture. Such films cannot be recommended for groups or individuals interested in learning about Hinduism, or for that matter, any of the religious traditions noticed in passing.

Monthly Ancestral Offerings in Hinduism
   8 minutes, color, 16mm, 1969
   Sale $100.00, Rental $8.00
   H. Daniel Smith—Image India
   Film Marketing Division/Film Rental Library
   Syracuse University
   1455 East Colvin Street
   Syracuse, NY 13210
   Also available from UIowa, WashSt, UWash, UWisc

This film depicts the tarpana offerings performed by Hindus to satisfy the needs of the ancestors, or "fathers." The ritual, occurring each month on the new-moon day (amavasya), is conducted on the roof of a middle class Sri-Vaishnava Tengalai brahman home in the city of Madras with the aid of the family religious teacher (acharya). Explained in the narrative and accompanying user's guide are the celebrant's self-purification prior to the ritual, the laying out of a grid of darbha grass as a "seat" for the visiting deceased, the offerings of sesame-seed water to maternal and paternal ancestors of both sides of the family, and the greeting of the ancestors by the celebrant. The ritual concludes with payment to the priest who oversees the ceremony.

Comments: The film focuses tightly on the details of an important rite surviving from Vedic religion, and one not previously filmed. The narration is clear and detailed and places the rite in the context of Hindu doctrine. Two recent studies of offerings to ancestors may complement the film: *An Indian Pilgrimage: Kashi* in the University of Wisconsin film series, and *Death and Rebirth in Hinduism* in the Exploring the Religions of South Asia video series, both reviewed in this section.

Murugan
   23 minutes, color, 16mm, 1976
   Sale $300.00, Rental $40.00
   Yvonne Hanneman
   Focus International, Inc.
   505 West End Avenue
   New York, NY 10024

This film depicts public highlights of a twenty-five-day festival celebrated in Jaffna (Sri Lanka). The god is Murugan (historically associated with Subramanyam, Skanda, Karttikeya, and Kumara), a deity popular in South India whose cult is prominent among Tamils in Sri Lanka. Shown here are colorful and memorable sequences including processions and varieties of personal acts of devotion—with remarkable footage on fire-walking—and a ratha festival with hundreds of men carrying a huge chariot.

Comments: This is one of several films now available for learning about the cult of the popular South Indian god Murugan—see also *Floating in the Air, Followed by the Wind; Pankuni Uttaram: Festival of Fertility; Skanda-Sasti: A Festival of Conquest;* and *Yakam: A Fire Ritual in South India.* . . . This one is particularly useful for demonstrating the presence of this growing cult in Sri Lanka, and for giving a vivid portrayal of the popular mass response to such ceremonies and public functions.

Pankuni Uttaram: Festival of Marriage and Fertility
   20 minutes, color, 16mm, 1970
   Sale $225.00, Rental $25.00
   Fred Clothey—South Indian Festivals series
   Professor Fred Clothey
   Department of Religious Studies
   2604 Cathedral of Learning
   University of Pittsburgh
   Pittsburgh, PA 15260

Depicted here are highlights of an annual, one-week celebration in the village of Palani in South India. The festival marks the marriage of Murugan (Subrahmanyam), an event which attracts half a million pilgrims each March/April to this popular hill-shrine—one of the five sacred sites of an ancient and still-growing cult. The film shows both the official liturgies which occupy professional priests, musicians and other religious specialists, and the variety of activities of the multitudes drawn there by the spectacle of processions, possessions, and pious acts of extreme devotion.

Comments: This film is an authentic, informed interpretation of Hindu religious practice, with an excellent account of cultic details, although perhaps too advanced or too technical for some unprepared viewers. The film requires considerable advance preparation for best utilization. Instructors and independent viewers will find detailed direction in the excellent (but demanding) essay which is available from the filmmaker.

Pilgrimage to a Hindu Temple
    14 minutes, color, 16mm, 1969
    Sale $150.00, Rental $12.00
    H. Daniel Smith—Image India
    Film Marketing Division/Film Rental Library
    Syracuse University
    1455 East Colvin Street
    Syracuse, NY 13210
    Also available from UMo, UWash

A middle-aged Tengalai brahman man visits the temple at Sriperembudur, twenty-five miles south of Madras in South India. This is the town where Ramanuja, the famous Sri-Vaisnava philosopher-saint, was born in the twelfth century, and the date is the celebration of the saint's birth. The pilgrim is shown bathing and then entering the temple. He proceeds through the chambers of the temple moving clockwise and inward until he reaches the inner shrine and makes his offerings. The narrative and user's guide stress this as "a journey of self-discovery and spiritual renewal."

Comments: The film accurately emphasizes the individual nature of Hindu pilgrimage, and the details of the inner chambers and shrines of a typical Hindu temple are combined effectively with the devotional experience of the solitary devotee. But this solitariness is also somewhat misleading and perhaps romanticized. What is missing is the noise, confusion, earthiness of a temple in festival times such as this. A good supplement is the film *An Indian Pilgrimage: Ramdevra* and a treatment of pilgrimage in South Asia in general is provided in *Hindu Pilgrimage* in the Exploring the Religions of South Asia series.

Sathya Sai Baba: His Life is His Message
 30 minutes, color, 16mm, 1973
 Sale $275.00, Rental $30.00
 Richard Bok
 Sathya Sai Baba Center & Bookstore
 7911 Willoughby Avenue
 Los Angeles, CA 90046

This devotional film wholly accepts the works and life of this contemporary personality-cult figure (b. 1926) of South India. He is presented as the miracle-working avatar his Indian followers claim him to be. Memorable footage in this film includes documentation of the diminutive Baba's proclivity for vibhuti-ashes where he is shown producing them by a circular motion of the hand, shaking them from an upturned pot, causing them to accumulate on his pictures, even though wide distances separate him and the phenomenon. As well, there is a shot showing "amrita" flowing from a small photograph of Baba. Accurately depicted are his style of public appearances and the enormous crowds of followers he has in India.

Comments: Visually alert viewers will be annoyed by the frequent reversal of images the film editor has permitted in his final print (Baba's mole is on his left cheek, not the right; he produces vibhuti-ashes with his right hand, not with his left); trained Indologists will be put off by the narrator's mispronunciation of words, as well as by such lapses as calling Bharata "the land of Attachment." All must be forewarned that the presentation dissimulates—e.g., Baba is said to come from a "pious, middle-class family" as a way of making clear his brahmin origins. On the whole, however, this is an impressive and useful presentation of this popular Indian "miracle man." Other films by the same filmmaker include: *Celebration* (70 minutes), *The Lost Years of Jesus* (92 minutes), and the 1980 release *Sai Baba: The Early Years* (30 minutes). For other related films, see the Topical Index under Personality Cult and Sathya Sai Baba.

Sectarian Hinduism: Lord Śiva and His Worship
 30 minutes, color, ¾ " videocassette, 1975
 Sale $45.00
 David M. Knipe—Exploring the Religions of South Asia
 Department of South Asian Studies
 1242 Van Hise Hall
 University of Wisconsin—Madison
 Madison, WI 53706

The first part of this film depicts two widely popular symbols of the Hindu god Shiva—the upright phallic form known as the linga and the image of the recumbent bull Nandi. The striking polarities of

Shiva's character and Shiva worship are surveyed in the second part of this program. Attention is also given to Parvati, Shiva's consort, and to Ganesha, Shiva's ubiquitous son. A third part of the program shows how worship of Shiva is performed in a contemporary temple in Banaras. The fourth section surveys the different kinds of shrines, temples, and sectarian communities throughout India generated by the worship of this extraordinary divinity.

Comments: This remarkably rich and versatile resource is useful as introductory material, as recapitulatory review, as enrichment of the study of Hindu myths, and as an example of Hindu sectarian developments. The presentation is highly recommended.

Sectarian Hinduism: Lord Vishnu and His Worship
30 minutes, color, ¾″ videocassette, 1975
Sale $45.00
David M. Knipe—Exploring the Religions of South Asia
Department of South Asian Studies
1242 Van Hise Hall
University of Wisconsin—Madison
Madison, WI 53706

This is an introduction to that "profound amalgamation" of Vedic, indigenous, non-brahmanical elements now coalesced into the deity known as "Vishnu." The first section presents historical, textual, and archeological evidence for reconstructing what may have been early forms of worship of this deity, followed by the various postures and attendants which characterize this deity's depiction. A third section focuses on the ten avataras (incarnations) of the Cosmic Lord, in particular Krishna, Rama, and on their companions. A final section provides some glimpses of Srirangam and Khajuraho, pilgrimage sites in the Vaishnava tradition.

Comments: While this program lacks the coherence and conviction of some of Knipe's other videotapes, it is nonetheless useful for a recapitulation of miscellaneous materials important for an introduction to Vishnu and his worship. And, most importantly, it demonstrates the breadth of the phenomenon of Vishnu-worship—more than is guessed at after a one-time reading of the *Bhagavad Gita.*

Sectarian Hinduism: The Goddess and Her Worship
30 minutes, color, ¾″ videocassette, 1975
Sale $45.00

**David M. Knipe—Exploring the Religions of South
Asia**
Department of South Asian Studies
1242 Van Hise Hall
University of Wisconsin—Madison
Madison, WI 53706

This program explores the "power and energy of the universe" recognized as "the Goddess" (devi). More than merely the mate or consort of one of the great male gods such as Vishnu or Shiva, the shakti-manifestation is more comprehensively to be understood as an ancient, pervasive, yet elusive, identity given to sacred powers of bursting fertility, vibrant energy, and primal matter. The goddess when personified represents the fecund and teeming universe which has quickened and nurtured the vibrant Hindu religious imagination. Sita, Sarasvati, Parvati, Lakshmi, Durga, Kali, and Sitala are among the many female deities representing the great and mysterious theme of the Goddess. The conclusion of the film presents two recent figures regarded as incarnations of the goddess—Ananda Mayi Ma and Sarada Devi.

Comments: This film is a sophisticated and thought-provoking presentation. It is most useful for advanced students already familiar with some of the major forms of Hindu piety and with some of the major figures of Hindu mythology.

The Serpent Deities: Art and Ritual in South India
18 minutes, color, 16mm, 1976
Clifford Jones—Traditional Art & Ritual in South India
Inquire: Clifford Jones
South Asia Center, Columbia University
New York, NY 10027

This shows a ritual in the worship of serpent deities filmed on location in the low-caste Pulluvan community of Kerala. The worship, in which women play a very active role, involves inducing two young, prepubescent, bare-chested girls to become spiritual mediums. They are encouraged to enter the trance state while seated in an elaborate mandala of five powdered colors in an intertwining snake pattern, situated beneath a mandapam. Music and dance are used to enhance the ritual. In trance, the girls dance in spirals sweeping away the mandala with brooms of straw. A second mandala is drawn featuring the image of the demon Bhutamas, and again the girls, having been asked if the deities are satisfied, destroy the image and tear down the straw birds and coverings of the awning. Details of the construction of both images are shown.

Comments: This is a vivid, colorful, and important film, but one that will not be pedagogically successful unless considerable background information is provided. For a further understanding of the themes in the film, and of regional Hinduism (Kerala), this might best be shown with one or more of its companion films in the series—*The Goddess Bhagavati* or *The Worship of the Deity Ayyappan* (reviewed elsewhere in this section)—and/or *Kamban Ramayana* or *Kuttiyattam* (see Part Two).

Skanda-Sasti: A Festival of Conquest
  17 minutes, color, 16mm, 1970
  Sale $225.00, Rental $25.00
  Fred Clothey—South Indian Festivals series
  Professor Fred Clothey
  Department of Religious Studies
  2604 Cathedral of Learning
  University of Pittsburgh
  Pittsburgh, PA 15260

This film depicts a festival occurring yearly in South India celebrating the victory of Skanda (Murugan/Subrahmanyam) over the force of evil embodied in the demon Sasti, followed by his marriage to the goddess (depicted in the film *Pankuni Uttaram* . . . in the same series). The film gives close attention to the rituals, pageantry, and social milieu of the popular holy celebration. The high point of the public events is a reenactment of the battle between the demon and Skanda, in which the demon is symbolically transformed when vanquished in the jousting.

Comments: Like other films in this series, the ritual complex is very difficult to grasp simply by watching the film and attending to the narration (which is at times difficult to follow). The public events are well filmed, and will sustain the interest of even uninformed groups, but in general the film is most important as a visual record of important aspects of the seven-day ritual. It thus serves as a supplement to the guide/monograph which supplies considerable detail and explanation of the ritual and the importance of Skanda. This film provides a valuable balance to the more general film *Murugan* by Yvonne Hanneman which shows the public ceremonies, and the film *Floating in the Air, Followed by the Wind* which shows the individual acts of devotion of the Murugan cult; it also should be seen in the context of the other two films in the series: *Yakam* and *Pankuni Uttaram*.

Swami Karunananda: From Wallaroo, Australia
  28 minutes, color, 16mm, 1971
  Sale discontinued, Rental $19.00
  Yavar Abbas—India Called Them
  New York University Film Library
  Washington Square, 41 Press Annex
  New York, NY 10003

The locale of this film is Rishikesh where, more than three decades ago, Sivananda founded his Divine Life Society and where, some years later, he accepted an Australian man for discipleship. This film is a profile of Swami Karunananda, depicting his life at the ashram, his expertise in Hatha Yoga methodologies, and his total renunciation of his former self and commitment to his new vocation.

Comments: The film honestly raises—and leaves curiously and subtly unanswered—the question of whether this is flamboyant play-acting or genuine commitment. It might be pedagogically useful to show this film along with another—Abbas' other film, *Maharishi Mahesh: Jet-Age Yogi*, or Hartley's *Evolution of a Yogi* (both reviewed in Part Three)—or the film *Swami Shyam*, reviewed below.

Swami Shyam
  20 minutes, color, 16mm, 1977
  Sale $220.00, Rental $5.00
  Film Australia—Asian Neighbours series (India)
  Australian Information Service
  Australian Consulate General
  636 Fifth Avenue
  New York, NY 10020

This film is about an English-speaking swami ("teacher") in the northern-most reaches of India and his entourage of devoted followers, mostly young adults from England and North America. Swami Shyam good-naturedly reveals his regimen to the camera. He explains that what he works for in his students is "that they should grow in that awareness with which they should become healthy, happy, at peace, and full of strength, [and manifest] sympathy, kindness for others, and help them. . . . " He is shown seated in meditation with his students; emerging from an outhouse, whereupon he launches into a brief dissertation on piles; taking a (warm) bath, all the while singing. Some of his English and American students speak of their satisfaction in learning from the swami. The film ends as the swami urges the camera crew to meditate, explaining the advantages derived therefrom.

Comments: This is a valuable glimpse of Neo-Hinduism, replete with implications relating to contemporary personality cults, particularly those which respond to the needs of Western youth seeking spiritual realization of Hindu wisdom. Swami Shyam construes his title to mean he is both "teacher and friend" to them; accordingly, he urges them to do "their own thing," and sprinkles his talk about the meditative life with such phrases as "a trip [that] is total," and being "tuned in with our energy," along with the vocabulary typical of English-speaking Hindu spiritual teachers of the modern period. His jolly and ready laughter is reminiscent of Maharishi Mahesh Yogi's. Indeed, this film nicely complements the treatment found of Mahesh Yogi in *Maharishi Mahesh: Jet-Age Yogi* by updating what is seen there, and it also bears comparison with *A Contemporary Guru: Rajnish.* (For other related films see the Topical Index under Guru and Yoga.)

Trance and Dance in Bali
    22 minutes, b/w, 16mm, 1951
    Sale $135.00, Rental $9.50
    Gregory Bateson and Margaret Mead
    New York University Film Library
    Washington Square, 41 Press Annex
    New York, NY 10003
    Also available from UCB, UCLA, NoIll, UIowa, UKans, UMich, UMinn, UNoCar, UUtah, UWash, UWisc

This is a 1937-1939 film by Bateson and Mead on a remarkable Balinese ceremonial dance dramatizing the cosmic polarities of life and death. In the conflict between the witch and the dragon, actor-dancers achieve a state of trance and turn their krises (sharp-pointed steel daggers against themselves. In the early stages of the ritual dance, the death-dealing witch enchants young girls into spreading plague, killing newborn babies, etc., reminiscent of the disease goddesses of folk Hinduism. Kris-bearing warriors attack the witch-goddess, whose glance withers them. Two by two they attack; she does not resist, but her effortless power subdues them into convulsive trance states. A priest revives them to a somnambulistic state, but still they are in trance. Women with krises also go into trance and, contorted in agony, turn their krises against their chests. The men in trance seizures do the same. Incense then calms them and those who become too violent are disarmed by the onlookers. So strong is the pressure of the point against the breastbone, the krises are seen to bend into permanent L-shapes, yet no one is hurt. The last part of the film constitutes a revival of the dancers (including the man who played the part of the witch-goddess) from trance states. Holy water and incense are used and offerings are made.

Comments: This is a landmark effort in the history of ethnographic film, and remains a rare and remarkable documentary on an aspect of folk religion in Balinese Hinduism. Virtually nothing of Indian Hinduism is evident, yet the scholar with a knowledge of folk Hinduism in South Asia (e.g., of disease goddesses) will perceive myth-ritual connections and perhaps some thematic South Asian origins. The trance-dance itself, however, is uniquely Balinese.

Vishnu's Maya
  30 minutes, color, 16mm, 1976
  Sale $350.00, Rental $45.00
  Thomas Ball
  Phoenix Films, Inc.
  470 Park Avenue South
  New York, NY 10016
  Also available from WashSt

This film presents a staging of the parable of Narada, who goes to Vishnu for instruction, and while performing a chore becomes involved in completely worldly existence, including marriage and family life. Finally, events of nature force a reawakening; Narada then realizes the illusory quality of phenomenal existence. The entire film was shot on location near the Ganges.

Comments: Though the source of the story (recounted, for example, by H. Zimmer in *Myths and Symbols in Indian Art and Civilization*, pp. 32–34) may not be readily found in ancient texts, this highly romanticized parable is authentically Hindu and pedagogically effective. This dramatization contains fine cinematography and is well acted by Benaras Hindu University professors of music and arts, although some viewers may find the Indian accent difficult to follow. The film is also useful as an idealized portrayal of the worldly functions of a village brahman priest. Interestingly, the viewer is caught up, like Narada in the myth, by the myriad details of society, rituals, economics, and politics.

Vṛndavan: Land of Kṛṣṇa
  24 minutes, color, 16mm, 1978
  Sale $295.00, Rental $30.00
  (Also available in Super-8 reels and cassettes, as well as in video-cassettes)
  The International Society for Krishna Consciousness
  The Bhakivedanta Book Trust
  3764 Watseka Avenue
  Los Angeles, CA 90034

This film is presented in three parts. In the first section, before the title appears, the camera focuses first on an icon of Krishna, "the Supreme Personality of Godhead," and then on contemporary ISKCON paintings of other related figures while the narrator recapitulates what we know of the Lord's life and career in Vrindavana "from the ancient histories of India which date back more than 5,000 years." A switch to shots of nature settings and of pilgrims in and around the town of Vrindavana characterizes the second section. The narration states that for believers there is "no place more holy" than Vrindavana and its "5,000 temples," where "all 30,000 inhabitants are devotees" of Him. Prominently featured here are shots taken in the ISKCON International Center, including footage of the guest house and interior precincts of its shrine. The third (and longest) section is an unhurried, and unsystematic, presentation of certain aspects of Krishna's teachings and his devotees' practices. The Lord's teachings are equated with the "natural" life of his peasants who work "not with technology but with the land's natural gifts." It is pointed out that the simple ways of Krishna which had been revealed 5,000 years ago were reiterated only 500 years ago when the Lord incarnated himself again, this time in the "disguise" of Lord Caitanya. A brief summary of Caitanya's life provides an opportunity for the film to catalogue various holy sites honored by the visitations of both Caitanya and by his earlier presence as Krishna. It is said that the "Science of Krishna Consciousness" was established in the early sixteenth century by the Goswamis; their realizations and rules of worship have been passed down to this day through an unbroken line of spiritual successors. Various acts of piety characteristic of the Krishna Consciousness Movement are intercut in this final third of the film. Near the end of the presentation it is stated that the "transcendental exchange between Krishna and his devotee is tangible and real, but for non-devotees it remains a mystery."

Comments: This is an attractive and accurate presentation of the type of Vishnuism centered on Krishna-bhakti espoused by Caitanya (1486-1534) and promulgated today by the Gaudiya school. Users are cautioned that other studies and materials are needed to present a balanced view of the god Krishna. This film is not only limited to one sect of Hinduism, but to one sect of Krishnaism. It magnifies Krishna as cowherd boy, a hero, a brother, a god—never as a lover, the role that occupies so prominent a place in Indian literature, dance, drama, music, not to mention religion. While "Krishna and his boyfriends" are mentioned, the gopis (cowherd girls) go unmentioned, and Radha is referred to only once in passing. Accordingly, this film—and indeed, any materials produced by ISKCON—must be used with caution appropriate to any confessional, sectarian presentation. Further, there are a number of actions depicted, mostly relating to worship, for which no attempt has been made to offer explanation or identification. Thus the viewer at some crucial points is given controversial interpretation; at others, insufficient information. As for usage of this film, it would seem advisable to reserve it a place in any course in which extended treatment is given to Krishna-bhakti. For courses in which shorter time is spent on Krishnaism, or in which it is imperative to give more widely ranging treatment of devotion or of other aspects of Hinduism, other films must be sought (for which see the Topical Index).

The Wages of Action: Religion in a Hindu Village
    40 minutes, color, 16mm, 1980
    Sale $200.00, Rental $25.00
    Jointly produced by the BBC's Open University and the University of Wisconsin's Department of South Asian Studies
    Department of South Asian Studies
    1242 Van Hise Hall
    University of Wisconsin—Madison
    Madison, WI 53706

Filmed in February 1979 in the village of Soyepur, near Banaras, this documentary focuses on the everyday religious practices of the different castes in Soyepur. It includes a wide range of puja activities, interviews concerning ghosts and how they must be placated, examples of spirit-possession and spirit-cure, a multicaste Satyanarayana-puja, a one-day pilgrimage to a nearby religious shrine, and a discussion by a brahmin housewife regarding how she maintains the ritual cleanliness of her kitchen.

Comments: This recent film was received too close to press time to permit review by members of the panel.

Wedding of the Goddess
    Part I: 36 minutes, color, 16mm, 1975
    Sale $155.00, Rental $20.00
    Part II: 40 minutes, color, 16mm, 1975
    Sale $170.00, Rental $20.00
    Mira Reym Binford, Michael Camerini, Joseph Elder
    Department of South Asian Studio
    1242 Van Hise Hall
    University of Wisconsin, Madison
    Madison, WI 53706

The first part of this film is largely background information concerning the famous Chittarai festival occurring during the months of April and May in Madurai, South India. The stories of Minakshi's wedding and the founding of Madurai are given through explanations of the various temple paintings. The film illustrates the importance of the seventeenth-century Nayak kings and local history in determining the form and style of the two rituals celebrating Minakshi's wedding to Shiva and the coming to Madurai of Minakshi's brother, Alagar, a manifiestation of Vishnu. The film emphasizes the importance of the temples to Minakshi and Alagar in folk Hinduism in the Madurai area. Part Two provides a day-by-day chronicle of the Chittarai festival, showing both the festival of Minakshi and her wedding to Shiva. The footage also depicts the festival procession of Lord Alagar to the edge of the city and back to his rural temple. Other scenes in the film include drawing a diagram of the Vastu Mandala, initiation with branding into a trance-like stage, and large crowd scenes in which people spray Lord Alagar with water in fulfillment of vows. Still shots from paintings and sculptures and filmed interviews with festival participants add other interesting dimensions to the film.

Comments: The two parts of this highly informative and visually attractive film can be shown separately, but are more effectively shown together. The film is also useful for showing the interplay of politics and local tradition in the dynamics of a religious festival. The initiation with branding compares well with *The Hindu Sacrament of Surrender,* and the wedding of the goddess Minakshi is comparable to the wedding of another South Indian god, Murugan, shown in *Pankuni Uttaram.* . . . [Note: A Minakshi Temple is currently under construction in Texas. For details write: Meenakshi Temple Society, P.O. Box 2345, Prairieview, TX 77445.]

The Worship of the Deity Ayyappan: Art, and Ritual in South India
    20 minutes, color, 16mm, 1976
    Clifford Jones—Traditional Art & Ritual in South India
    Inquire Clifford Jones
    South Asia Center
    Columbia University
    New York, NY 10027

This film concentrates on the artistry of rituals in the Tiyattu ritual cycle celebrating the worship of Ayyappan. As in the first film in the series, *The Goddess Bhagavati,* an image is constructed with the powders of five symbolic colors, to the accompaniment of tantric rites and music. There is a complex ceremonial dance resulting in trance, during which the priest (identified by the narrator as a shaman) walks back and forth through the hot embers of a fire, ritually destroys the colored-powder picture, and performs as an oracle. Attention is given in the film to the place of the ritual in this Kerala religious community.

Comments: This presentation is very colorful and well filmed, and is an important glimpse at the powerful combination of music, symbolic art, and dance in the achievement of trance in Indian religious practice. It is important to note that the fire-walker is an adept at this ritual, and not an untrained ecstatic. The films in this series are vivid, and a general audience may respond well to them, but if they are to provide an effective learning experience they should be shown only after considerable advance preparation on ritual, symbolism, and trance. The films in this series may well be viewed together, while this particular film might also accompany *Floating on the Air, Followed by the Wind,* and *Himalayan Shaman.* . . . A guide to the film is in preparation and will be most welcome.

Yakam: A Fire Ritual . . .
  10 minutes, color, 16mm, 1970
  Sale $175.00, Rent $15.00
  Fred Clothey—South Indian Festivals series
  Professor Fred Clothey
  Department of Religious Studies
  2604 Cathedral of Learning
  University of Pittsburgh
  Pittsburgh, PA 15260
  Also available from UWash

This film follows the details of the complex procedures in an annual series of ritual fire offerings to the god Skanda (associated with Subrahmanyam/Murugan). Within an inner-temple sanctum, the priests consecrate themselves and the offering chamber and then proceed to offer 101 symbolic oblations into the altar fire. The film sets the ritual in the larger setting of the Skanda-Sasti festival (see the film *Skanda-Sasti* . . . in the same series), held yearly at the Tiruchendur temple on the Bay of Bengal in Tamil Nadu (Madras State).

Comments: This film provides the most detailed account of ritual in any of the films by Professor Clothey. It tries to bring out the influences and interaction of Vedic, tantric, and ritual medicinal practices in Hindu tradition. Each step of the ritual is detailed in the monograph prepared to accompany the film, as are the important aspects of consecrating the chamber and the officiants. The complexity of the ritual and its compression through the medium of film make it virtually essential to study the guide closely, and see the film repeatedly, if the processes of the ritual are to be understood.

Slides and Filmstrips

The Bhagavad Gita Illustrated
   31 slides, color
   Sale $30.00
   International Society for Krishna Consciousness
   The Bhaktivedanta Book Trust
   3764 Watseka Avenue
   Los Angeles, CA 90034

This set of slides illustrates the ideals of the *Bhagavad Gita* as they are interpreted by the International Society for Krishna Consciousness, otherwise known as the Hare Krishna movement. The slides are of paintings by contemporary devotees and are in the style of printed publications of the sect—bright, glossy, and devotional. The text supplies commentary and verses of the *Bhagavad Gita* translated by A. C. Bhaktivedanta Swami, founder of the energetic ISKCON cult. In addition to the scenes of Arjuna, Krishna, Dhritarastra, and the opposing armies, there are imaginative renderings which depict the types of beings according to what they eat and types of worship. The universe contained in Krishna's Lotus, the body, and all of Krishna's manifestations (including Shiva and Indra) are also shown. Students seeing the slides for the first time deserve to be informed of the faith-context in which they originated.

Fabric of India: Religion in India
   50 slides, color, 1970s,
   Sale $50.00
   Henry M. Ferguson
   Joan Ferguson
   5 Chestnut Hill North
   Loudonville, NY 12211

All but seven of these slides pertain to Hinduism. Several examples of the following are given: temples (Chidambaram Siva temple, Birla temple in Delhi, Durga temple in Banaras); shrines (in homes, at a pipal tree, by the wayside); priests and wandering ascetics; temple carts and processions (Kanchipuram, Tiruchirapulli, Thanjavur, Dussehra festival in Delhi); puja and worship (tulasi plant, garlands, powdered colors, dedicating a school, blessing a shop); pilgrims and ghats; wedding couples; with a name-day ceremony rounding out the collection. There is a paragraph of discussion for each slide, with suggested topics as "religion," "festivals," "avatar," "the arts." The discussion of the scenes in the guides provides little specific information about them. The effectiveness of the slides varies from quite good (e.g., #8 household shrines, #34 wedding ceremony), to decidedly poor (e.g., #44 Dussehra procession, #36 pilgrimage, #43 bathing ghats). The quality of reproduction is good.

Hindu Rituals
  Color filmstrip, programmed audiocassette, 1978
  Sale $20.00
  Teacher's Guide (23-page, soft cover) $3.75
  Produced by Lee Smith and Wes Bodin with Joan Voight and Pat Noyes for the World Religions Curriculum Development Center, Minneapolis, MN
  Religion in Human Culture Series: The Hindu Tradition—Hindu Rituals (Series No. 15526)
  Argus Communications
  7440 Natchez Avenue
  Niles, IL 60648

This eighteen-minute, programmed filmstrip provides a very rapid survey of Hindu rituals, commencing with brief attention given to festivals, vows and pilgrimages, domestic prayers and worship. Main focus, however, is on the life-cycle rituals (frames #19–88: pre-natal through post-mortem samskaras, or sacraments, with ample treatment both of thread investiture and of marriage). Like its companion filmstrip in this Argus series, *Introduction to Hinduism* (q.v.), this presentation was prepared mainly for primary school and junior high students; more sophisticated students will perhaps find the narration inadequate to their levels of interest because the explanation given of the activities displayed is so abbreviated. There is no reason, however, that the visuals in this filmstrip cannot serve a resourceful college-level instructor as the basis for a classroom presentation utilizing his/her own more informed explanations for the frames. The filmstrip, with the teacher's guide—which not only reproduces in print the narration but also provides additional data— may also serve students well in independent study assignments on the topic of Hindu rituals. The only other comparable visuals readily available on these rituals in one package is the AAR-sponsored slide set *India—Hinduism* (in some cases, providing more visual data and explanatory details; in others, less).

Most of the pictures used in this filmstrip were provided by Professors David M. Knipe and H. Daniel Smith, and are available in another format in the former's videocassettes—*The Life Cycle in Hinduism: Birth, Initiation, Marriage* and *Death and Rebirth in Hinduism*—and in the latter's film *Hindu Sacraments of Childhood . . .* and slide set *India—Hinduism*. All of these are reviewed elsewhere in this section.

Hinduism
  2 color filmstrips with cassette
  Sale $40.00
  7 filmstrips with 4 cassettes
  Sale $98.00
  Adapted by Henry M. Ferguson
  Social Studies Schools Service
  10000 Culver Boulevard
  Culver City, CA 90230

This is one of seven filmstrips in the award-winning Religions of India series (others include Buddhism, Islam, Sikhism, Jainism, Christianity, and Zoroastrianism). The lecture and guide are pre-collegiate level, but do supply useful notes for the individual frames which include temples, home and village shrines, private and public worship (especially good), images of major deities, along with a few gratuitous cartoons and pictures of the elements. The generalizations in the notes are misleading, still this is a credible visual scan of Hinduism, more suited to independent study than the classroom. This is available for sale only with the companion strip on Buddhism.

Hinduism
  140 slides, color, 1952
  Sale $75.00
  Kenneth W. Morgan
  Visual Education Service
  The Divinity School, Yale University
  409 Prospect Street
  New Haven, CT 06511

This slide survey of Hinduism includes a selection of temples, primarily in South India, with exterior and interior views, processions, rites, priests, worshippers, ascetics, and temple cars; shrines in North and South India; bathing scenes in Banaras; priests, worship in the home; life-cycle rites, limited to marriages and cremations; a selection of typical images in regional shrines, temples, and households. There is a forty-page guide. This slide set was the first of its kind and after almost thirty years is still a valuable resource, although it should be augmented with contemporary materials, particularly in the areas of ritual and personal worship.

Hinduism—A Vignette

25 slides, color, 1970
Sale $25.00
C. Kulkarni
Scholarly Audio-Visuals, Inc. (Formerly Sheikh Publications)
5 Beekman Street
New York, NY 10038

This collection of slides is accompanied by a lecture on Hinduism with a short introduction and a discussion of the material covered by the slides—pictures of images and practices in good quality reproductions. A record of the lecture is also available. (This is one of a series of slide-lectures also covering Sikhism, Jainism, Zoroastrianism, Islam, and Buddhism.)

Holy Places of India
Part I: The North
Part II: East, Central, West and South
  Part I: 50 slides, color
  Sale $50.00
  Part II: 58 slides, color
  Sale $58.00
International Society for Krishna Consciousness
The Bhaktivedanta Book Trust
3764 Watseka Avenue
Los Angeles, CA 90034

These two sets provide 108 slides on a number of important pilgrimage spots, particularly those held sacred by devotees of Krishna. The views are generally very good, well photographed and appropriate to suggest the place. In the North are shown Badrinatha, Hrisikesh, Hardwar, Kurukshetra, Mathura, Vrindavana, Naimisaranya, Ayodhya, and Allahabad (including shots of Kumbhamela). Across the rest of the country, Varanasi (Banaras), Puri, Pushkar, and Shri Rangam receive special attention among the twenty-three sites depicted. Each slide and site receives careful attention in the eighteen pages of notes that accompany the slides. Doctrines held by the International Society for Krishna Consciousness have in some few instances influenced the selection of sites and festivals, as well as the notes (Shiva = the destructive manifestation of Vishnu). None of these prevents this dual set of slides from presenting an exceptionally good overview of pilgrimage sites and the acts of devotion, entertainments, art and architecture, and festivals which make up such an important part of public Hinduism.

India—Hinduism
  160 slides, color
  Sale $52.00
  Charles Kennedy and H. Daniel Smith
  Visual Education Service
  The Divinity School, Yale University
  409 Prospect Street
  New Haven, CT 06511

This set of slides includes historical material, a survey of Hindu images and monuments, and detailed coverage of ceremonial and personal ritual activities. Slides #1-15 Indus Valley civilization; #16-34 Hindu deities; #34-45 morning rituals; #46-61 domestic rituals; #62-90 life-cycle and sacraments of childhood; #91-96 investiture; #97-101 marriage; #102-111 final rites; #112-120 pilgrimage places; #121-140 pilgrimage activities; #141-145 representative sites; #146-160 nineteenth- and twentieth-century Hindu figures. The accompanying text includes a fifty-page scholarly explanation of the slides that is quite useful. There are also brief appendices on general resources for South Asian studies, recordings and slides available, and an extensive appendix on films. Many of these slides are of scenes from Professor Smith's Image India series. This is the most comprehensive and useful single collection of color slides on Hinduism currently available. The collection of colored slides is of uniformly good quality. Users of the film series Image India may wish to use these slides in class discussions to provide quick visual recall of the films. (The set with text in French is also available on request.)

Introduction to Hinduism
  Color Filmstrip, programmed audiocassette, 1978
  Sale $20.00
  Teacher's Guide (19-page, soft cover) $3.75
  Produced by Lee Smith and Wes Bodin with Joan Voight and Pat Noyes for the World Religions Curriculum Development Center, Minneapolis, MN
  Religion in Human Culture Series: The Hindu Tradition—Introduction to Hinduism (Series No. 15525)
  Argus Communications
  7440 Natchez Avenue
  Niles, IL 60648

Clearly designed for social studies courses at the primary school and junior high levels, this fifteen-minute, programmed introduction to Hinduism touches in passing upon India's history and social organization, Hinduism's basic beliefs, and the abiding concern among devout believers for the sacrality of certain times and special places, as well as the continuing sense among thoughtful Hindus of the divine presence in icons depicting popular deities. The teacher's guide, which reproduces the generally commendable and colorful photos in black and white, prints out the narrator's script in case the instructor prefers to serve as narrator with a voice more familiar to his or her students. It also provides additional data for consideration, as well as some comments about visual details seen in the photos.

The same critique which applies to panoramic treatments of Hinduism in motion pictures (see above review of *The Hindu World*) applies with equal force to generalizing filmstrip presentations. A fifteen-minute presentation on Hinduism must necessarily defy specifics, cannot possibly do justice to the complexity and subtlety of the living traditions, and hence is inevitably distorting and misleading. However well-intentioned and professionally researched the present filmstrip under review, it must be deemed inadequate largely due to its broad-ranging conception. Much more successful are treatments tending toward the monographic approach—see, for example, the companion filmstrip in this same series *Hindu Rituals* (above).

The Life of Sri Caitanya
  51 slides, programmed audiocassette and script, 1977
  Sale $50.00
  The Bhaktivedanta Book Trust
  3764 Watseka Avenue
  Los Angeles, CA 90034

Near the beginning of this presentation it is promised that the viewer will be given "a brief glimpse into Caitanya Mahaprabhu's miracles, theology, and social philosophy" (slide #3). What is in fact provided is an uncritical rehearsal of some hagiographic legends associated with the life of Caitanya (1486-1534), with his closest associates and followers, and with some sites made sacred by his memory. Only incidentally are some devotional practices of Gaudiya Krishna-bhaktas treated; virtually nothing substantial is offered by way of theology or social philosophy. Yet the set contains some visuals of sites, bazaar depictions of saintly figures, cultic icons *in situ,* and pertinent ISKCON studio paintings relating to the Brahma-Madhva-Gaudiya-Sampradaya to which instructors may find it useful to expose their students—especially if the learning goal is greater comprehension of Krishnabhakti in Bengal or the origins of the ISKCON movement.

Puri—The City of Lord Jagannatha
  40 slides, color
  Sale $40.00

The Bhaktivedanta Book Trust
3764 Watseka Avenue
Los Angeles, CA 90034

This set of slides provides a glimpse of Puri at festival time with interesting pictures of temples, images, the making of images, offering of flowers, ritual paintings on the ground, crowd scenes, and pictures of the chariot being pulled. The level of photography is generally good, the reproduction is professional. A useful guide gives a paragraph on each slide.

Slides of the Ramayana
  40 slides, color, 1977
  Sale $12.00
  Donald and Jean Johnson
  New York University Asian Studies Education Project
  Washington Square, 735 East Building
  New York, NY 10003

This set is now available in preliminary form, and consists of slides showing a variety of classical, artistic, and contemporary popular-style renditions of the major episodes of the Sanskrit epic. The accompanying guide provides a quick summary of the Ramayana story, and a description of the slides includes information on the style of the paintings and interpretation of the scenes depicted.

The Story of Krishna
  40 slides, color, 1976
  Sale $16.00
  Donald and Jean Johnson
  New York University Asian Studies Education Project
  Washington Square, 735 East Building
  New York, NY 10003

"This slide-essay has been prepared for high school and college students and is intended to present one aspect of Lord Krishna—The Divine Herdsman." The booklet accompanying the slides gives an introduction to the different aspects of Krishna and ends with a "Teaching Strategy" aimed at the teacher or independent learner. The body of the text is the script for an available twenty-minute tape. There is also a section, "The Parable of Krishna," which uses the same visual material for a more philosophical and analytical discussion. The aspect of Krishna treated in the slides is his life in Vrindavan as a child and cowherd. The narrative (also available on tape) is an uncritical recension of the stories of Krishna's youth. Many of the slides are paired with translations of devotional poetry from Dimock and Levertov's *In Praise of Krishna*, and from Archer's *The Loves of Krishna in Indian Painting and Poetry* (which seems to have inspired this slide set). Even though most of the slides are Kangra paintings, and many are taken from books, this is not an art set. The reproduction of the slides is good.

Vrindavana: Land of Krishna
  60 slides, programmed audiocassette, script, 1977
  Sale $60.00
  The Bhaktivedanta Book Trust
  3764 Watseka Avenue
  Los Angeles, CA 90034

This set of sixty slides is meant to supplement, not merely to parallel, what is shown in the film of similar title (q.v.), likewise produced by the increasingly active audiovisual division of the International Society for Krishna Consciousness (the so-called "Hare Krishna People"). The locale is the same as the film, but the treatment differs; this format provides stationary shots of temples and icons, holy places and devout pilgrims for more reflective viewing. Three groups of slides comprising the bulk of this presentation may be noted in particular: a group which specifies the contributions of Caitanya and two of his six Goswami followers to the task of restoring and rebuilding Vrindavana (slides #7-18); another group which points out particular holy spots which are geophysically associated with significant mythic events in the story of Krishna's nativity and career in and near Vrindavana (slides #19-34); and a third group which characterizes the professions and pastimes of Vrindavana inhabitants today (slides #37-54). While almost everything that is said in criticism of the film also applies to this set of slides, instructors who prefer using slides over films in class will nonetheless find this a useful and reasonably priced learning resource.

The World's Great Religions: Hinduism
  2 filmstrips (117 frames) with audiocassette, 1973
  Sale only $50.00
  Teacher's Guide and Student Materials by David Wale
  Time-Life Multimedia
  100 Eisenhower Drive, P.O. Box 644
  Paramus, NJ 07652

This set is an updated version of the earlier Time-Life series. It includes many splendid visuals including some from issues of *Life* magazine as well as others very similar to photos in the *Time-Life Cook Book*. Most of the visuals are not described in the taped lecture;

instead, they serve as illustrations—almost as if they were pictures gracing the cookbook. The narrative attempts to give an overview of Hinduism up to modern times, and takes considerable pains to avoid reinforcing common stereotypes of Hindu superstition and Indian poverty. The rudiments of the Hindu stages of life, religious education, and caste are well treated. Unfortunately, the narrator makes a number of mistakes in pronunciation (e.g., the sacred syllable "aam"). Throughout most of the soundtrack, there is in the background a well-selected series of excerpts from Indian religious music—including a brief Vedic passage, flute music, Baul songs, group singing, and instrumental music—for the most part, cued to appropriate parts of the narrative.

Recordings

OFTEN OVERLOOKED BY instructors seeking to convey the spirit of Hinduism to students is the phenomenon of sound in Indian culture. The bardic word, the chanted verse, the saintly utterance, the musical phrase—all have played enormously important functions in the dissemination (and shaping) of the Hindu tradition. The following list is by no means exhaustive; it is intended to help the neophyte identify some available recordings to use as instructional resources. For additional recordings currently being marketed, see below.

The Bengal Minstrel—Music of the Bauls
　　Produced by Peter K. Siegel, notes by Charles Capwell
　　Nonesuch Records
　　665 Fifth Avenue
　　New York, NY 10022

A wandering minstrel who has become a Calcutta fixture, Purnachandra Das performs six songs in the Baul tradition, accompanied by his entourage. Included are songs to Bengal holy places, to Krishna, and expressing his longing for union with Krishna. A rough translation of each song is given. The notes discuss the symbolism and musicology of the songs. The introduction traces the roots of the Baul tradition to a fusion of Saktism, Buddhism, Sufism, and Vaishnavism—a view supported by contemporary scholarship.

The Bhagavad Gita
　　Text notes by Dr. S.R. Ranganathan, 1951
　　Folkways Records
　　43 West 61st Street
　　New York, NY 10023

Only the first band of Side One is the *Bhagavad Gita.* Here Book Two, verses 54-72, are expertly chanted by T.M.P. Mahadevan. The other half of Side One is the reading of an English translation (provided in the notes) by Swami Nikhilananda. The translation is reasonably accurate but the reading is difficult to follow. Side Two is readings from Valmiki's *Ramayana* (in Sanskrit). The recitation is somewhat uneven. The second selection may be of special interest to religion classes. In this passage, Brahma reveals the true nature of Rama and Sita as manifestations of Vishnu and Lakshmi (from Yuddha Kanda, chapter 117). The notes present readable translations and transliterations of the texts. However, they are very poorly reproduced.

Chants Religieux Du Bengale—Religious Songs from Bengal
   Recorded by Deben Bhattacharya and Shri Nabagopal
   Mitra Thakur; notes by Deben Bhattacharya
   Boite à Musique
   133 Boulevard Raspail
   Paris VI, France
   or:
   Record and Tape Sales Corporation
   95 Christopher Street
   New York, NY 10014

On one side of this record are four typical Baul songs. The other side is a portion of a performance of kirtanas (devotional poem-plays) devoted to Krishna, such as are often sung throughout Bengal. The selections are compositions of the North Indian bhakta Chandidas whose works are cherished among the greatest of North Indian vernacular religious poetry. Such performances might last several days and are an important part of Bengal's religious communal life and literature and art. (Note: this selection is approximately the same as band 4 on the recording of *Songs of Krishna*, also produced by Deben Bhattacharya, but no longer available). This record, taped in 1954, is issued with notes in both French and English explaining and translating each song. (Deben Bhattacharya is the author of a volume of translations with an introductory essay, *Love Songs of Chandidas*, New York: Grove Press, 1970, Evergreen paperback, E542. $2.95)

Dhyanam/Meditation
   Produced by Peter K. Siegel, notes by Robert E. Brown—Nonesuch
   Explorer Series H72018
   Nonesuch Records
   665 Fifth Avenue
   New York, NY 10022

Five short works of South Indian devotional music are sung by K.V. Narayanaswamy. The works recorded are by religious poet-musicians from around the nineteenth century. The first band of Side One is a kriti by a famous Tamil poet, Gopala Krishna Bharatigar. The second is by the renowned Telugu saint-poet Tyagaraja (1767-1847), praying: "O Raghuvara, is it proper for you to forget me?" Side Two includes a kriti in Sanskrit to Krishna and ends with songs in the jhawali and tillana styles, lighter modes associated with the devotional dance, Bharatanatyam. The notes give the composers' dates and translations of the passages sung, but do not elaborate on the religious significance of the music. The recording is clear and representative.

The Four Vedas
    2 records, 4 bands
    Recorded by J.F. Staal and John Levy; notes by J.F. Staal—Asch
    Mankind Series
    Folkways Records
    43 West 61st Street
    New York, NY 10023

This two-record set deliberately includes styles and selections *not* found in the UNESCO collection of *Vedic Recitation and Chant* (see below) which contains the most common pieces. Hence, in many ways this record may be used for more intensive study as well as to complement the UNESCO collection. The notes are much more extensive and the translations are quite good. Staal takes pains to explain the differences between the textual traditions of the North and South of India. The entire second disc is devoted to the traditions of the Nambudiri community of Kerala on the grounds that it is a strong tradition and not easily accessible in recordings. (This is the community whose performance of the Agnicayana ritual was recorded in the film *Altar of Fire* by Robert Gardner and Staal.) This recording also includes a number of instances of group singing and also a selection where boys are being taught to recite. Like the UNESCO recording, the present album includes a number of "Vikriti" recitations (patterns of repeating syllables and words within a passage), and the opening hymn of the Rg Veda (to Agni) is a feature of both albums.

Hindu Chants (Yoga Mantras for Spiritual Communion)
    Record or cassette, 1970
    Performed by Swami Shiva Premananda, English translations by Edwin H. Kaplan
    Scholarly Audio-Visuals, Inc.

5 Beekman Street
New York, NY 10038

This recording consists of "mantras" chanted by Swami Shivapre-mananda, a representative of Sivananda Yoga-Vedanta Centers. The recordings of his recitation of unidentified Sanskrit verses alternate with readings of approximate English translations. The diction is clear and somewhat musical, the selections are arranged according to such categories as "shanti mantras," "guru mantras," "arpana mantras," "swasti mantras," and "mantras for japa." This classification is simply by purpose or use of the mantras suggested by the Sivananda sect. Roughly translated, these are chants used for calming oneself, for praising the guru, for dedicating oneself, for making blessings, and for repeating over and over. This is not a universal scheme for classifying mantras. The sound quality is poor, and the notes are very scanty and uninformative. Potential users may find it useful to compare this with *The Sounds of Yoga Vedanta*, noted below.

Indian Street Music/The Bauls of Bengal
   Produced by Peter K. Siegel—Nonesuch Explorer Series H72035
   Nonesuch Records
   665 Fifth Avenue
   New York, NY 10022

Six songs are sung by Hare Krishna Das, Lakshman Das, Purnachandra Das, and Sudhananda Das, personal compositions addressing the Lord Krishna, or referring to yoga or to the religious life of the sadhu. The notes supply approximate translations and are helpful for understanding the symbolism. The introduction stresses Rabindranath Tagore's interest in the Bauls, and their place in modern Bengali culture.

Meera Bhajans
   M.S. Subbulakshmi—*Meera Bhajans* EALP #1297
   Lata Mangeshkar—*Meera Bhajans* ECSD #2371
   Peters International, Inc.
   619 West 54th Street
   New York, NY 10019

These are devotional songs composed by Mira Bai, the loved and revered poetess-saint of fifteenth-century North India, a princess who gave up everything for Krishna. Her devotional songs are sung throughout north central India. Two recordings are currently avail-

able with this title. One is sung by M.S. Subbulakshmi, the most
renowned female classical vocalist of post-independence India. Her
renditions are in the highest artistic tradition. The other recording is
by Lata Mangeshkar, the best-loved popular singer of modern Hindi
film and radio. Her playback singing is the sine qua non of successful
films in India, and her voice, more than any other, has shaped
contemporary Indian taste. For authenticity, Subbulakshmi's version
must be heard; for contemporary Hinduism, Lata's singing would be
the most likely to be found in a North Indian home. Playing both
records for comparison is recommended. The notes for the two
recordings are too brief to be helpful. Those for Subbulakshmi's
recording do give brief descriptions of the bands.

Musical Atlas Bengal
  UNESCO Collection—Musical Atlas Series
  UNIPUB
  345 Park Avenue South
  New York, NY 10010

The first ten minutes of Side Two of this record present a performance of the "Dasavatara" (the ten avatars of Vishnu) perhaps the
best-known verses from the enormously popular Sanskrit devotional
poem *Gita Govinda* by Jayadeva. Listening to this recording of the
"Dasavatara," together with reading an English translation of the *Gita
Govinda* (such as Barbara Miller's *Love Song of the Dark Lord*,
Columbia paperback, 1977), would give an interesting illustration of
the importance of music, dance, art, and literature in bhakti. Other
bands on the record include three Baul songs by Purnachandra Das; a
kirtana, dialogue song of Radha's reconciliation with Krishna; and a
boatman's song devoted to Krishna. Notes are in English, French, and
Italian, and provide basic information on the instruments and types of
music presented.

Religious Music of India
  Folkways #4431
  Recording and notes by Alain Danielou and Kenneth W. Morgan
  Folkways Records
  43 West 61st Street
  New York, NY 10023

Recorded by Alain Danielou in 1951 at a time when he was freely
accepted in many Hindu temples as a devotee, this still remains an
exemplary recording for the teaching of music in Hinduism. The
record includes: a bhajana and vina solo sung and played by Swami
Parvatikar, a wandering ascetic who never uttered a sound except to

sing religious music; Vedic chanting correctly done by Pandit Ramji Shastri Dravida in the ancient, orthodox manner; Hymn to Shiva sung by Sri T.M. Krishnaswami Iyer, famous master of South Indian-style singing; and Rama Lila, an example of the popular singing of stories from Hindu epics, sung by a high priest of a temple in Banaras; and Bengali kirtanas. These selections were made by Alain Danielou from a large collection of tapes to serve as an introduction to Hindu religious music, either in a classroom or for independent study. The choice is apt, the notes are clear and provide both translations and transliterations as well as approximate transcriptions of the tunes. Most importantly, the religious significance of each performance is made explicit.

Ritual Music of Manipur
   Recording and notes by Louise Lightfoot
   Folkways Records
   43 West 61st Street
   New York, NY 10023

The Manipur Kingdom in far eastern India (on the east side of Bangladesh, north of Burma) was converted to the Chaitanya Sect of Vaishnavism more than two centuries ago. Their music includes combinations of imported Bengali bhakti music and ceremonies mixed with their indigenous traditions. Now Manipuri dance is considered among the finest of Indian religious dances. The recording provides an ideal mixture of archaic and modern Hindu ritual. The notes provide basic ethnographic information and black-and-white photos. Each band is briefly described, with references to the dances or other events that properly accompany the music. The recorder of the music has written *Dance Rituals of Manipur, India* (Hong Kong, 1960).

The Sounds of Yoga Vedanta
   Ethnic Folkways #8970, 1966
   Recording and notes by Leslie Shepard
   Folkways Records
   43 West 61st Street
   New York, NY 10023

Swami Sivananda (1887-1963) was a spokesman for Neo-Hinduism and a founder of the Divine Life Society. The Yoga Vedanta Forest Academy at Rishikesh carries on his teachings in an ashram setting. This disc records a day at the Ashram. First, the sound of the river Ganges; then some voices chanting "Om namo Narayana" and "Ram, Ram, Ram." In the background, someone is performing abhishekha (sprinkling water ritual) on a Shiva linga. Later in the day, the current successor to the late Sivananda's leadership position in the movement is about to give darshan. A devotee shouts praise in Hindi and Sanskrit to the guru, then all recite prayers. As the Swamiji drinks coffee he speaks of worldly matters (Band 4), and bids goodbye to Leslie Shepard who is making the recording. The next band includes some chanting and the sound of over a hundred people eating. Side One concludes with more group chanting ("Hare Rama, Hare Krishna"), followed by a lecture on Yoga Vedanta ideals (in English), followed by more chanting.

Side Two includes good musical performances on the rudra vina, and an unidentified Ashram singer performing Kirtan. More group recitations of mantras, and a closing arati-ceremony, professionally chanted, complete the recording.

The quality of the recording is good. Both for the merely curious and the initiate the record gives insight into the particular practices that make up the spiritual day at the Sivananda Ashram. The recording comes with a pamphlet of descriptive notes. For another example of a recording originating within the Sivananda movement, see *Hindu Chants* reviewed above. For visual glimpses into ashram life in India and elsewhere, see the Topical Index.

Vedic Recitation and Chant
UNESCO Collection—Music of India Album, Record I
Recorded by Alain Danielou
UNIPUB
345 Park Avenue South
New York, NY 10010

This album includes examples of recitation and chanting of passages from the Rg Veda, Yajur Veda, and the Sama Veda. The first two bands repeat an invocation to Kubera, once spoken and once sung. The third band is the very first hymn of the Rg Veda, the hymn to Agni, the God of Fire. (This is also recorded—chanted in a different style—on the record by J.F. Staal, *The Four Vedas*, above). There are seven recordings of passages from the Sama Veda and four from the Yajur Veda, including a hymn to Prajapati, the Lord of Creatures, found in the important text *Satapatha Brahmana*. All but two of the sections were recorded in Banaras from 1949-1951, with a variety of styles and traditions represented. The album includes condensed but helpful notes in English, French, and German, and translations and transliterations of the texts.

CHAPTER 2

Cultural Background for the Study of Hinduism

Films and Videotapes

FROM VARIOUS SOURCES, there may be as many as 400 to 500 films focusing on various aspects of the subcontinent—on cities, on demography and geography, on dance and the performing arts, on industrialization—and the panel has by no means screened them all. We have made an effort to include films which have noticeable relevance to the contextual background against which Hinduism as a religion has developed and may be gainfully taught.

Apu Trilogy: Pather Panchali; Aparajito; The World of Apu
   115 minutes, b/w, 16mm, 1955
   Rental $85.00 (minimum)
   113 minutes, b/w, 16mm, 1956
   Rental $85.00 (minimum)
   106 minutes, b/w, 16mm, 1959
   Rental $85.00 (minimum)
   Satyajit Ray
   Audio Brandon Films, Inc.
   34 MacQuesten Parkway South
   Mount Vernon, NY 10550

This classic trilogy traces the struggles, tragedies, and commitment to life of a typical Bengali family with a sensitivity which has established Ray as India's foremost film director. Whether seen separately or as a trilogy, these are superb films—and an excellent presentation of living Hinduism.

Asian Earth
   J. Michael Hagopian
   Atlantis Productions, Inc.
   1252 La Granada Drive
   Thousand Oaks, CA 91360

Also available from ArizSt, UIll, UMo, UNeb, SyrU, KentSt, OklaSt, USoCar, BYU

A study of a village family in their unending effort to wrench from the earth enough food for nourishment; to arrange their affairs to insure security. Although the narration is not suitable for college-level audiences, the visuals are rich and evocative of many aspects of daily life in rural India. Included are brief sequences pertinent to interests in piety in the home, cremation, and so forth. Filmed almost twenty years ago, the filmmaker recently returned to the same village and is now preparing for release *Asian Earth: The New Generation*. The two films shown together may be expected to generate considerable post-screening discussion for instructors whose learning goals include ethnography, modernization, and the like.

Balasaraswathi
    20 minutes, color, 16mm, 1963
    Sale $200.00
    John Frazer
    Center for Arts
    Wesleyan University
    Middletown, CT 06457

Filmed at a private performance in the early sixties when Bala-saraswathi was Dancer in Residence at Wesleyan University, this short film captures something of the presence and artistry of India's most respected exponent of the classical Bharata Natyam dance of South India. Its authentic music and delicate reflection of mood, each in its way evocative of the spiritual power of this form of dance as a religious event, combine to make this a remarkable documentary. (A more recent film, *Bala*, a profile of the dancer by India's famous filmmaker Satyajit Roy, includes the performance of "Krishna Nee Nagane Baro" and an entire varnam. This thirty-three-minute color film, made in India in 1977, is currently awaiting an American distributor.)

Bali Today with Margaret Mead
    18 minutes, color, 16mm, 1969
    Sale $225.00, Rental $30.00
    Elda Hartley and Margaret Mead
    Hartley Productions, Inc.
    Cat Rock Road
    Cos Cob, CT 06807
    Also available from KentSt

The emphasis is on the arts in Balinese village traditions, with brief and uninformed attention to Hinduism. Only late in the film come authentic glimpses of cremations, ancestral offerings, and a wedding. Potential users are advised that, in addition to the two films on Bali reviewed elsewhere in this volume—*Trance and Dance . . .* (Chapter One) and *Miracle of Bali* (this chapter)—additional films currently being marketed may prove useful. These are: *Bali: Isle of Temples* (27 minutes, Centron Films, 1973); *Bali: Religion in Paradise* (29 minutes, ABC, 1973); and several short films on Bali produced by Film Australia.

Banaras
   22 minutes, b/w, 16mm, 1972
   Sale $140.00, Rental $15.00
   Michael Camerini
   Department of South Asian Studies
   1242 Van Hise Hall
   University of Wisconsin—Madison
   Madison, WI 53706
   Also available from UMo, WashSt

This film presents effectively and poetically the sights, sounds, rhythms, and moods of the holy city of India, with attention to worship at shrines, in temples, and on the bathing ghats. The musical background, without narration, allows the viewer to receive authentic impressions of Banaras. For a similar treatment of Calcutta, see *Portrait of a City;* of a village, *Gazipur;* of two villages, *Indian Village Life*, all reviewed elsewhere in this section.

Bhismallah Khan
   28 minutes, b/w, 16mm, 1967
   Sale $165.00, Rental $9.50
   James Beveridge and Tom Slevin
   Audio-Visual Center
   Indiana University
   Bloomington, IN 47401
   Also available from UCB, IndU, UWash, UWisc

This film portrait of the renowned Indian Muslim virtuoso is set entirely in Banaras. The film tries to put shehnai music into its Hindu religious and cultural setting. It includes footage of the ghats, street scenes in Banaras, musical training of children, unusual shots of a traditional Hindu wrestling arena and gymnasium, shehnai performances in temples, and marriage processions.

James Beveridge has made several other films on Indian musicians, one of which is reviewed elsewhere in this section—*Music of North India: Four Indian Musicians.* Two parts of this film ("Bhimsen Joshi" and "Pandit Jasraj") are available only through the Arts Center at Wesleyan University, Middletown, CT 06457. Other films featuring Indian musicians are *Dhrupad, A Musical Tradition in Banaras,* and *Raga,* also reviewed in this section. Attention is also called to Philip P. Kavan's fifty-minute film *Khansahib: Usted Ali Akbar Khan in America* from Western World Productions, P.O. Box 3594, San Francisco, CA 94119. For other films depicting music and musicians, see the Topical Index.

Bhoodan Yatra
22 minutes, b/w, 16mm, 1950s
See Appendix I: Sources of Audiovisual Materials under India, Govt. of . . . , for nearest distribution center of this film.

This is a composite of newsreel footage closely following Vinoba Bhave's foot pilgrimage around India (beginning in 1951), inspiring the giving of millions of acres of land for the landless and carrying the message of Sarvodaya (universal uplift) to the nation. Even Jayaprakash Narayan is briefly present in this historic footage. Bhave provides a direct link between Gandhi and the recent ruling government of India. The print viewed was in poor condition.

Calcutta
99 minutes, color, 16mm, 1968
Sale $900.00, Rental $90.00
Louis Malle for BBC
Pyramid Films
Box 1048
Santa Monica, CA 90406
Also available from UCB, Purdue, IndU, UMinn, USoCar, UWash

This documentary film was considered derogatory and offensive by the Indian government. The narrative and film editing do strongly emphasize overcrowding and poverty, and may tend to reinforce many widely held prejudices and negative conceptions of India. However, the camera work is memorable and visually stimulating, and there is a lengthy though poorly explained sequence on the activities associated with Durga puja.

Cave Temples—Hindu

11 minutes, b/w, 16mm, 1950s
M. Bhavnani and P. Nurami
See Appendix I: Sources of Audiovisual Materials under India, Govt. of . . . , for nearest distribution center of this film.

While the narrative of this film makes rash and misleading statements, still this may be used for its fine footage of Hindu religious sculpture of the late classical times in a number of caves. The sculpture is beautifully filmed and correctly identified, with some attention given to myths and deities represented, as well as to such art-historical stylistic marks as coiffures and ornaments.

Courtship
60 minutes, b/w, 1962
Sale $330.00, Rental $30.00
National Film Board of Canada
1251 Avenue of the Americas
New York, NY 10020
Also available from UCB, UCol, FlaSt, NoIll, SoIll, UMinn, PennSt

The courtship patterns of four cultures—Sicily, Iran, Canada, and India—are examined. The fifteen-minute section on India records negotiations of a fatherless Kerala Shaivite family to arrange the eldest son's marriage. It is sufficiently rich in ethnographic details to elicit questions about family life, social relationships, freedom and authority, and love and marriage. Good for enrichment purposes.

Devi
96 minutes, b/w, 16mm, 1961
Rental $75.00 (minimum)
Satyajit Ray
Audio Brandon Films, Inc.
34 MacQuesten Parkway South
Mount Vernon, NY 10550

A haunting film by Satyajit Ray about an elderly Bengali widower who dreams his daughter-in-law is an incarnation of the Goddess ("Ma," the beneficent aspect of Kali). He begins to worship her in his simple faith, but the girl's life is brought to a tragic end when she can no longer sustain the ordeal her spreading fame thrusts upon her. Increasingly treated as an object of worship, literally idolized and the recipient of daily puja, she loses her mind and commits suicide. The film raises interesting discussion possibilities about the role of religion, the extremes of bhakti, and obedience to elders.

Dhrupad
  50 minutes, color, 16mm, 1974
  Virendra Kumar Jain with Sheldon Rochlin
  Inquire, Navin Kumar, Inc.
  967 Madison Ave.
  New York, NY 10021

  Virtuoso vocal performances by N. Zahiruddin Dagar and Fayi-
zuddin Dagar, members of the Dagar family, renowned as preservers of
Dhrupad (an elegant classical style of North Indian devotional music),
are recorded in this film. Some attempt is made to reveal the religious
content of Dhrupad. Except at the beginning—where an unfortunate,
misleading statement which associates Dhrupad with the 5,000-year-
old [sic.] Vedic tradition of mantras—the presentation contains no
narration. Instead, trick photography and animation interspersed
with footage of Banaras ghats, temples, and religious paintings are
used to indicate the religious content of the verses and the exalted
meditative state of the performers. The songs include praises to Vishnu
and Shiva. For other films treating Indian musicians, see *Bhismallah
Khan*, *Music of North India . . .* , *A Musical Tradition in Banaras*,
and *Raga*, all reviewed elsewhere in this chapter.

Discovering the Music of India
  22 minutes, color, 16mm, 1969
  Sale $275.00, Rental $18.00
  Bernard Wilets
  B.F.A. Educational Media
  2211 Michigan Avenue, P. O. Box 1795
  Santa Monica, CA 90406
  Also available from ArizSt, UAriz, FlaSt, USoFla, NoIll, IndU,
  IowaSt, UIowa, UKans, UMinn, UNeb, SyrU, KentSt, SoCar, BYU,
  WashSt

  This film introduces with immediacy and charm not only Karnatic
(southern) and Hindustani (northern) forms of Indian music, but also
identifies and demonstrates several Indian musical instruments, as
well as explaining and performing some basic elements of a Bharata
Natya dance repertory. The obvious studio setting does not detract
from the artistry of the performers nor the commendation they deserve
for succeeding in their difficult task of addressing themselves to people
totally unfamiliar with the South Asian musical arts.

Distant Thunder
  100 minutes, color, 16mm, 1973
  Rental $125.00
  Satyajit Ray
  Cinema 5—16mm
  595 Madison Avenue
  New York, NY 10022

Satyajit Ray's color feature film focuses on life during the Bengal famine. The struggles of a poor Brahmin and his wife to eke out a living appropriate to their caste status, the interaction of caste and money in village Bengal, and the impact of famine, war, and modernization under the British on traditional Indian values are all beautifully and poignantly portrayed.

Festival Time
  16 minutes, color, 16mm, 1973
  See Appendix I: Sources of Audiovisual Materials under India, Govt. of . . . , for nearest distribution center of this film.

A Madhya Pradesh panorama following the seasons with rustic scenes and festivals, including Raksha Bandhan, Janmasthami, Ganesh Chaturthi, Dussehra, Diwali, Id, Kumbhmela at Ujjain, Republic Day, Shivaratri, Muharram, and Holi. This film is on the cultural activity of festivals and holidays, and not at all on religious "significance." Still, despite the simplistic narrative and film design, it does give quick visual impressions of the major holidays in their proper sequence in the year.

Gandhi
  27 minutes, b/w, 16mm, 1958
  Sale $160.00, Rental $15.00
  CBS—Walter Cronkite
  Contemporary/McGraw-Hill Films   1221 Avenue of the Americas
  New York, NY 10020
  Also available from UCB, FlaSt, NoIll, UIll, Purdue, IndU, BU, UMich, UMinn, UMo, SyrU, KentSt, OklaSt, PennSt, UTex, WashSt, UWisc

As an authoritative and memorable presentation of Gandhi's life and significance, this film is second only to the eighty-minute version *Mahatma Gandhi: Twentieth Century Prophet.* It contains footage of the Salt March (1930), the trip to England (1931), Independence Day (1947), and Gandhi's death (1949).

Gandhi
   25 minutes, color, 16mm, 1977
   Sale $325.00, Rental $30.00
   Profiles in Courage series
   Learning Corporation of America
   1350 Avenue of the Americas
   New York, NY 10019

This film, although the most recently produced of the four on Gandhi reviewed in this chapter (see *Gandhi*, above; *Mahatma Gandhi: Twentieth Century Prophet* and *Non-Violence—Mahatma Gandhi and Martin Luther King . . .* , below), is the least likely to succeed in class. Visually literate students at the college level are unlikely to be drawn into this dramatization. Although the improvised script touches upon some of the most provocative and compelling issues associated with this figure (especially from the perspective of the psycho-historian), the imaginary interview format, in which Patrick Wilson acts as interlocutor to a Gandhi figure impersonated by Lewis Negin, simply does not "work." While it is true that many in the current classroom generation have never even heard of the "Mahatma," and even though it may be argued that every effort should be made to penetrate this comtemporary ignorance, it is doubtful that the way to present the man Gandhi is by means of an actor wrapped in an obviously pinned-up sheet, wearing burnt-cork makeup, his front teeth blacked out, responding to questions patently fictive. Less audacious as an approach to Gandhi, and infinitely more satisfactory, are those treatments which utilize actual newsreel footage to mark the major events in his career.

Ganges River
   17 minutes, color, 16mm, 1955
   Sale discontinued, Rental $8.25
   Edward Levonian
   Audio-Visual Center
   Indiana University
   Bloomington, IN 47401
   Also available from UCt, FlaSt, SoFla, UIll, IndU, UMe, UMinn, KentSt, UUtah, WashSt, UWy

Tracing the river from its origin in the mountains to the mouth beyond Calcutta, this film attempts to show the river not only as a geophysical reality but also as a spiritual entity. This is one of three or four films on roughly the same topic; see the Topical Index.

Ganges: Sacred River
   27 minutes, color, 16mm, 1965
   Sale and Rental discontinued
   Encyclopaedia Britannica Educational Corp.
   425 North Michigan Avenue
   Chicago, IL 60611
   Also available from UAriz, UCB, UCol, FlaSt, UIll, IndSt, BU, KentSt, PennSt, SoCar

To many in India, the Ganges is the symbol of life. This film travels with the flowing waters from the source high in the Himalayas, through the plains, past pilgrims, along banks where ceremonies are performed, and finally into the sea. Preferable to older black-and-white productions, this still does not adequately address the importance of the Ganges in Hinduism.

Gazipur
   20 minutes, color, 16mm, 1975
   Sale $300.00, Rental $35.00
   Bruce Holman
   Interbook, Inc.
   13 East 16th Street
   New York, NY 10003

A colorful village panorama with no narration, but a fine sitar performance made especially for the film. A guide details the caste and occupation of the people shown. The footage covers harvest, women's work, activities inside small village houses, including eating and preparing meals, school scenes, and so forth. Armed with the user's guide and his own knowledge of caste and Hinduism, the teacher can use this film effectively (compare *Banaras, Gazipur*, and *Portrait of a City*, all reviewed elsewhere in this chapter.

God with a Green Face
   25 minutes, color, 16mm, 1972
   Rental $11.00
   Bruce A. Ward and Myron Emory for The American Society for the Eastern Arts at the California Institute of the Arts
   Academic Support Center Film Library
   The University of Missouri — Columbia
   505 East Stewart Road
   Columbia, MO 65211

   This film, which was presumably produced as a research tool for students interested in the performing arts of India, presents a learning potential for students of Hinduism. Members of the Kerala State Academy of the Arts are filmed performing a Kathakali ("story-dance") version of the *Ramayana*. Five excerpts are performed in an authentic bare-stage setting. First, Ravana appears disguised as an ascetic only to be transformed into his "terrific" form to kidnap Sita, and thence to battle with the winged Jatayu; next is the amusing shouting match and fierce battle between Bali and Sugriva, including the intervention by Rama to decide the fray; then comes the humiliation of Hanuman as prisoner before Ravana (after the monkey has located the captive Sita), and the resourceful monkey's escape and retaliation by setting fire to the kingdom of Lanka with his burning tail; thereupon is shown the grand encounter in battle between Rama and Ravana, ending in the latter's screeching death; and finally one sees the final triumphant coronation of Rama and Sita in a rain of flower petals. Prior to these excerpts, the all-male cast is shown preparing their elaborate makeup, donning their traditional costumes, and meditating before placing atop their heads their respective crowns which "transforms each actor into the epic character he portrays."

   This film captures the "mystery" and "romance" of a popular form the Hindu epic takes in South India. The photography features the predominant colors of reds, whites, and blacks; only occasionally does the screen yield to the green used on the faces of the main characters to denote their heroism. Instructors looking for other materials based on dissemination of the Rama-story in dance form are alerted to the section of the film *Miracle of Bali* . . . (q.v.) which shows a Balinese folk interpretation of part of the story.

Gurkha Country
   19 minutes, color, 16mm, 1966
   Sale $225.00, Rental 12.50
   John and Patricia Hitchcock
   International Film Bureau, Inc.
   332 South Michigan Avenue
   Chicago, IL 60604

   Intended as a "guide" for anthropological field work, this study of the Magars in a Nepalese mountain valley includes brief shots of shamans' rites and cures, the first feeding of rice to an infant, a wedding, and ritual payment to a guru. Magical practices and a form of puja to a goddess (represented by a small tree and stones) with chicken, rice, and turmeric offerings, comprise rare footage of tribal religious expressions that are an essential but seldom photographed dimension of Hinduism.

Holy Himalayas
12 minutes, b/w, 16mm
K.L. Khandpur and N. Bhavnani
See Appendix I: Sources of Audiovisual Materials under India, Govt. of . . . , for nearest distribution center of this film.

This old black-and-white film is unusual, if not unique, in showing the upper reaches of the Ganges and the pilgrim route north from Hardwar to Uttar Kashi: Kedarnath, Bhadrinath, and Tapovana lake. The emphasis is more on the scenery than on the pilgrimage, but it is one of the most sacred pilgrimage areas in Hindu India, cherished because of the beauty of the Himalayas. The print viewed was in poor condition.

Imminent Deities
31 minutes, color, 16mm, 1969
Sale $400.00
BBC Production
Time-Life Multimedia
100 Eisenhower Drive, P. O. Box 644
Paramus, NJ 07652
Also available from UIll, UWash

This film has many liabilities, but it does succeed in capturing the natural power felt at Mamallapuram ("Mahabalipuram") and in reflecting the stateliness of Tanjore, in both places lingering over the architecture and sculpture found there with some commendable attention to detail.

In India the Sun Rises in the East
14 minutes, color, 16mm, 1970
Rental $9.50
Richard Kaplan Productions
University of Washington
Seattle, WA 98195

An impressionistic kaleidoscope of scenes from all over India, presumably depicting activities which transpire among the many peoples of the subcontinent during the course of one day, this film starts out with sunrise, ends with sunset. In between are shown views of people going to work by different modes of transportation, people working at various tasks in diverse settings, people relaxing in a variety of ways. Materials visible in specific scenes, as well as the juxtaposition of selected sequences, occasionally places the modern and the primitive side by side.

This film, albeit somewhat unusual due to its good photography and its self-conscious abandonment of narrative format, is typical of numerous films which have little direct relevance to the teaching of Hinduism, even though the focus is on India. It is conceivable that instructors might use it and similar films, to good pedagogic ends so long as they are prepared to provide the necessary background.

Indian Village Life: Two Villages in Orissa Province
    16 minutes, color, 16mm, 1973
    Sale $230.00, Rental $23.00
    Julien Bryan
    International Film Foundation, Inc.
    475 Fifth Avenue, Suite 916
    New York, NY 10017
    Also available from PennSt

This film presents a visually attractive and informative view of the efficiency and complexity of day-to-day life in a fishing village and a farming village. There is no narrative or guide accompanying the film, and only one scene focuses on the religious devotions of a woman. However, the film may be very useful for the clarity with which it suggests the technical sophistication of traditional India. See also *Gazipur*, above.

An Indian Worker: From Village to City
    18 minutes, color, 16mm, 1977
    Sale $250.00, Rental $25.00
    Michael Camerini and Mira Reym Binford
    International Film Foundation, Inc.
    475 Fifth Avenue, Suite 916
    New York, NY 10017

This film is essentially a re-edited version of *Village Man, City Man*, and is made by the same team of filmmakers as the South Asia Film Series. This version is shorter and the narrative is geared to a non-specialist audience.

Invitation to an Indian Wedding
    20 minutes, color, 16mm

Ramesh Gupta
**See Appendix I: Sources of Audiovisual Materials under India,
Govt. of . . . , for nearest distribution center of this film.**
**[Note: This film is also available at no-rental charge from Public
Service Audience Planners, Inc., New York/Chicago/Holly-
wood. See Appendix I, ibid., for nearest address.]**

This film treats marriage as a contemporary social event with brief
nods to religion as tradition, custom or sacred fire, sacred chant, etc. In
brief skits, it covers the meeting of in-laws, checking horoscopes,
interviewing the bride and groom to be, and the like. The steps of a
wedding are outlined (not defined as to locale, caste, or sect), including
tying the thread, tying dhoti and sari together, and going round the
sacred fire. The level of narration is high-schoolish and the print
viewed was worn. Still, the film does suggest the social activities typical
of contemporary middle- and upper-class weddings.

Kailash at Ellora
20 minutes, b/w, 16mm, 1940s
Clement Baptista
**See Appendix I: Sources of Audiovisual Materials under India,
Govt. of . . . , for nearest distribution center of this film.**

This film succeeds in conveying the greatness of this enormous
temple dug out of a single stone outcrop. There are good technical
explanations of the temple construction. The Ramayana and the
Mahabharata friezes, the statues of Vishnu, Shiva, and others, and the
interior of the temple complex are well filmed. Unfortunately, the
prints currently available are more than twenty years old.

Kaleidoscope Orissa
35 minutes, color, 16mm, 1967
Sale $450.00, Rental $25.00
Pilgrim Films
International Film Bureau, Inc.
332 South Michigan Avenue
Chicago, IL 60604
Also available from UCB, UCt, UIll, BU, UMich, SyrU, UUtah

A well-made film that may be of more interest to students of arts and
handicrafts than of religion. This kaleidoscopic treatment of Orissan
crafts includes some information about caste employments, footage on
painting in the Vaishnava tradition, and the autumn ceremony of
Karttikeya (in which his image is constructed and then after a
procession, "drowned and abandoned to the waters").

Kamban Ramayana
  30 minutes, b/w, 16mm, 1974
  Clifford Jones—Traditional Art & Ritual in South India
  Inquire: Clifford Jones
  South Asia Center
  Columbia University
  New York, NY 10027

An important film on the religious theater in India, showing the setup and enactment of a shadow-puppet version of the South Indian Ramayana by Kamban.

Khajuraho
  20 minutes, b/w, 16mm, 1956
  Mohan Wadhwani, V. Shirali, and Zul Vellani
  See Appendix I: Sources of Audiovisual Materials under India,
  Govt. of . . . , for nearest distribution center of this film.

"Living evidence of the unseen hammers and chisels" of the eleventh-century Orissa, this old film treats these ornate abandoned temples as art and as a record of bygone civilization and only peripherally as religion. The erotic imagery of the sculpture is neither overlooked nor prominently displayed. The black-and-white camera work is excellent and very well blended with the background music and narrative.

Konarak
  21 minutes, b/w, 16mm, 1958
  Rishikesh Mukerjee and Hari S. Das Gupta
  See Appendix I: Sources of Audiovisual Materials under India,
  Govt. of . . . , for nearest distribution center of this film.

This old film shows the design and sculpture of the famous sun temple. It opens with air shots of Konarak and pilgrims on the beach, a pilgrim camp, and the start of their circumambulation of the temple. The camera then proceeds on its own, scanning sculpture of deities, maithuna figures (embracing couples), animals large and small. The temple is called the crowning achievement of Orissa temple architecture and the Black Pagoda. The camera work effectively shows many fine details of the sculpture and is especially apt for giving the narrative effect of the friezes.

Kucchipudi—Part One
  20 minutes, color, 16mm, 1973
  M.Y. Kulkarni and T.A. Abraham

See Appendix I: Sources of Audiovisual Materials under India, Govt. of . . . , for nearest distribution center of this film.

This film focuses on the traditional devotional dance-drama named after Kucchipudi village in Andhra Pradesh. While the film concentrates on the performance aspects of the dance and its preservation in modern times as a secular art, it does give information on the religious traditions of the dance and its poet-saint originators of the sixteenth century. Among the performances shown is a brief solo dance of the Dasavatara (ten avatars) and a fully staged dance skit of the story myth of Prahlada.

Kuttiyattam: Sanskrit Drama in the Temples of Kerala
   27 minutes, color, 16mm, 1974
   Clifford Jones—Traditional Art & Ritual in South India
   Inquire: Clifford Jones
   South Asia Center
   Columbia University
   New York, NY 10027

This unique film on a form of Sanskrit theater preserved by the temple community of Kerala discusses the place of the theater in the temple and shows the elaborate ritual preparation of the performers, including makeup. It concludes with footage of two live, full-costume performances.

Land of the Indus
   28 minutes, color, 16mm, 1974
   Sale $240.00, Rental $22.00
   John Frank and John Herr
   Center for Instructional Resources
   State University College of New Paltz
   New Paltz, NY 12561

This film moves down the Indus River in what is now Pakistan, showing ancient peoples and traditional lifestyles, and is important for several minutes on the excavations of Mohenjodaro and the Indus Civilization. Professor Frank has also brought out a set of slides on the Indus Civilization; these are reviewed elsewhere in this section (p. 108). For another film on the Indus Civilization, see *Pakistan: Mound of the Dead*, below.

A Look at the Castes
   52 minutes, color, 16mm, 1967-68
   Sale $795.00, Rental $75.00

Louis Malle—Phantom India
New Yorker Films
16 West 61st Street
New York, NY 10023

In spite of the highly editorialized cinematography and narrative, this film has useful footage illustrating Malle's thesis that caste is largely invisible unless you know what you are looking at. Although the various sequences are not well related, there is excellent camera work and an exceptionally good view (without any useful explanation) of a funeral and cremation and rites afterwards.

Madhubani Painters
    18 minutes, color, 16mm, 1971(?)
    S. Bannerjee and V. Shilli
    See Appendix I: Sources of Audiovisual Materials under India, Govt. of . . . , for nearest distribution center of this film.

Madhubani village in North Bihar, while typical of Indian villages in many respects, claims to be part of the Mithila of old where Sita and Rama were married. The women there have preserved a unique style of folk art: brightly colored paintings with bold two-dimensional designs of religious subjects. Ramayana and Krishna Lila scenes are popular. Details of completed pictures are shown and the manner of painting is portrayed. A colorful and agreeably narrated and filmed presentation.

Mahatma Gandhi: Twentieth Century Prophet
    82 minutes, b/w, 16mm
    Rental only, $40.00
    Ideal Picture Co.
    34 MacQuesten Parkway South
    Mt. Vernon, NY 10550
    Also available from SoCar

Of the half-dozen films on Gandhi, this is unquestionably the best: it includes a long passage on the Salt March (1930), and excellent footage of his funeral and memorial services. For a shorter version of comparable quality, see *Gandhi* (narrated by Walter Cronkite), reviewed above.

Miracle of Bali: The Midday Sun/Night/Recital of Music
    54/54/43 minutes, color, 16mm, 1972
    Sale and rental discontinued

BBC Production
Xerox Films
245 Long Hill Road
Middletown, CT 06457

A superbly filmed three-part presentation of the Balinese, "a
people intoxicated by the arts," with an attempt to portray "the
religious roots of all the arts." It emphasizes music, carving in stone
and wood, painting, and dance traditions, the last including lagong
dance-drama and the Ramayana-based monkey dance.

Mirror of Gesture
21 minutes, color, 16mm and videocassette, 1973
University of California Media Extension Center
Extension Media Center
University of California—Berkeley
Berkeley, CA 94720

Filmed entirely in the Indian galleries of the Los Angeles County
Museum of Art, this film uses elaborate zoom effects, with distracting
intercuts of placid images with a live dancer, ostensibly to show the
relation not only between Indian sculpture and dance but also between
the gestures of hands and fingers utilized symbolically in both media.
The film is overdone with cinematic mannerisms, its visual effects
fatiguing. It is not recommended inasmuch as it fails to serve either as
pedagogic guide to iconography and dance or as an aesthetically
refreshing film experience. The relations between it and the
thirteenth-century Hindu treatise on mudras by Nandikeshwara,
Abhinayadarpana ("Mirror of Gesture"), are incidental at best.

Music of North India: Four Indian Musicians
29 minutes each, color, 16mm, 1970
Sale $400.00 each, Rental $40.00 each
James Beveridge Associates
c/o Edna and Friends, Inc.
18 West 45th Street—Room 503
New York, NY 10036
[Note: The first two films—on Bhimsen Joshi and on Pandit
Jasraj—are available for rental from: Center for Arts, Wesleyan
University, Middletown, CT 06457.]

This set of four films includes portraits of the performances and
lifestyles of four musicians: Bhimsen Joshi and Pandit Jasraj, vocal-
ists; Vijay Rao, flute; and Amjad Ali Khan, sarod. The film on Pandit
Jasraj especially brings out the importance of religion as a source of

inspiration for music and for its sponsorship by the wealthy. Notes accompany the films, and a monograph with general background information on Indian music, produced by Marie Joy Curtis, is available from the New York State Education Department Bureau of Mass Communications.

A Musical Tradition in Banaras
  40 minutes, color, 16mm, 1974
  Sale $230.00, Rental $20.00
  Roger Hartman
  Department of South Asian Studies
  1242 Van Hise Hall
  University of Wisconsin—Madison
  Madison, WI 53706

This film sets the professional life of an Indian tabla player, Panchu Maharaj, in the larger context of his personal life. Filmed in Banaras and a nearby village, it includes interview footage and informal performances, as well as insights into his teaching and personal philosophy. For other films profiling Indian musicians, see *Bhismallah Khan; Dhrupad;* the four which comprise the series *Music of North India: Four Indian Musicians;* and *Raga*—all reviewed in this chapter.

Nepal: Land of the Gods
  "The Tantric Universe"
  22 minutes, color, 16mm, 1976
  Sale $290.00, Rental $50.00
  "Tibetan Heritage"
  19 minutes, color, 16mm, 1976
  Sale $290.00, Rental $50.00
  "Sherpa Legend"
  21 minutes, color, 16mm, 1976
  Sale $290.00, Rental $50.00
  (All three films: Sale $800.00, Rental $140.00)
  Mike Spera and Sheldon Rochlin for Dakini Productions
  Focus International, Inc.
  505 West End Avenue
  New York, NY 10022
  Also available from UMo

This is the title of a series of three films made in the Kathmandu and Kungu valleys of Nepal. Cinematographically, they are excellent films; however, the narrations in them are unimpressive and often quite erroneous. For the most part, the films focus on Buddhism, but

"The Tantric Universe" includes attention to the unique blend of Hinduism and Buddhism in Nepalese Tantrism. Images of Ganesha, Hanuman, Vishnu, and Shiva are shown, as well as animal sacrifices to Kali. These three films have been reviewed, individually and at some length, in the companion volume *Focus on Buddhism*.

Non-Violence—Mahatma Gandhi and Martin Luther King: The Teacher and the Pupil
   15 minutes, color, 16mm, 1971
   Sale $200.00, Rental $25.00
   C. Grinker and M. Koplin
   Pictura Films Distribution Corporation
   111 8th Avenue
   New York, NY 10011

This film effectively juxtaposes footage of the American civil rights movement, especially in Selma, Alabama, with footage of the Satyagraha movement. King's indebtedness to Gandhi is made explicit through his own speeches. Their views and their deaths by assassination are drawn out as parallels. A study guide is available.

North Indian Village
   32 minutes, color, 16mm, 1959
   Sale $390.00, Rental $17.50
   John and Patricia Hitchcock—Cornell University Film Center
   International Film Bureau, Inc.
   332 South Michigan Avenue
   Chicago, IL 60604
   Also available from ArizSt, UAriz, UCB, UCol, UCt, FlaSt, SoFla, IdahoSt, UIll, UIowa, BU, UMich, UMo, SyrU, NoCar, UTex, BYU, UUtah, WashSt, UWash, UWisc

A study of Khalapur, a village northeast of Delhi, with focus on the Rajputs. Of interest to the study of Hinduism are substantial footage on marriage and betrothal ceremonies, and briefer attention to a village temple, a Muslim saint's shrine, a Brahman's daily rites, an upanayana prelude to a marriage, and the festival of Holi. Excellent on caste roles, occupations, service exchanges (e.g., the regulation of social behavior in caste rankings at festivals), and women's lives and roles. Filmed 1953-1959.

On the Fringes of Indian Society
   52 minutes, color, 16mm, 1967-68

Sale $795.00, Rental 75.00
Louis Malle—Phantom India
New Yorker Films
16 West 61st Street
New York, NY 10023

This film provides interviews in and film footage of several small communities in India: Bondo Tribe, Toda Tribe, Syriac Christians, Cochin Jews, and the Aurobindo Ashram at Pondicherry. The interaction of the tribes with modernization and with Hinduism is discussed, and the disruption of their ways is indicated. The footage of the Aurobindo Ashram has a background of a barely audible recording of The Mother. An aged resident of the Ashram is interviewed and demonstrates his daily Hatha Yoga exercise.

Padma, South Indian Dancer
20 minutes, color, 16mm, 1977
Sale $220.00, Rental $5.00
Film Australia—Asian Neighbours series (India)
Australian Information Service
Australian Consulate General
636 Fifth Avenue
New York, NY 10020

Padma is a South Indian performer and teacher of the traditional Bharata Natyam dance form. In this profile film, she reflects on her "inward spiritual satisfaction" as a dancer, her vocation as a teacher, and her craft as a choreographer. There are brief sequences showing dance performances. The narrative explanations come from Padma herself who speaks on the relation of temple sculptures to dance poses, the variety of meanings attributable to the "pataka" hand-gesture, and her own artistic preference for "realistic" animation and imitation of life over the stylized gestures used by other traditional dancers. The film ends as Padma bids fond farewell to one of her most promising students, who departs to get married; it is suggested that she may perhaps carry on the tradition as a performer and/or as a dance teacher.

This film provides a useful glimpse into the behind-the-scenes operations and aspirations which characterize a modern-day school of the dance in urban South India, but it fails to explain the dance itself, either as an art form or in terms of its relation to traditional Hindu ideology. Nonetheless, the film may serve helpfully for such insight in that it does provide on dance as rigorous discipline, and on the closely knit relationship of teacher to student in this art form. For a similar treatment of the student-teacher relationship among musicians, see *Raga* (below). For another depiction of a traditional Bharata Natyam performer, attention is called to Satyajit Roy's documentary on the incomparable Balasaraswathi, *Bala* (33 minutes, color, 1977, still awaiting an American distributor at the time this review went to press), and also to *Balasaraswathi* (above). For a treatment of a more modernist popularization of the dance, as it has been co-opted by the Indian movie industry, see *Helen, Queen of the Nautch Girls* (30 minutes, color, 1972, available through New Yorker Films). In addition, several films on music education in India are available through Dr. Marie Joy Curtiss (see Appendix II-B: Sources for Additional Information), and from The Asia Society (ibid.), which has documented several actual dance performances by Indian artists during U.S. tours. Consider also *Discovering the Music of India,* reviewed above in this chapter.

Pakistan: Mound of the Dead
   27 minutes, color, 16mm, 1972
   Sale $495.00, Rental $49.50
   Chatsworth Film Distributors, Ltd.—People and Places of Antiquity series
   Centron Educational Films
   1621 Ninth Street, Box 687
   Lawrence, KA 66044

Here is a visually memorable and intelligently narrated tour of the unearthed city of Mohenjo-daro, "one of the greatest cities of the ancient world," long since vanished and "forgotten before the Roman Empire was born." The emphasis throughout is on the technological sophistication of the ancient Indian citizens of the cities abandoned so long ago. Although there are two or three lapses in the otherwise unobjectionable script, the film on the whole succeeds admirably in sustaining a sense of wonder at the achievements, a sense of mystery in regard to the eventual decline of the culture. An unforgettably vivid demonstration ends the film proposing that among the many contributing factors in the final disappearance of the civilization was "ecological disaster" brought about by deforestation, in turn caused by the ceaseless firing in brick kilns of the very building blocks which constituted the wonder of the cities. The inhabitants of Mohenjo-daro "plundered their own environment . . . [and the forests which once represented] the natural resources of the Indus Valley literally went up in smoke." With the film's forceful ending, preceded by the haunting photography among the ruins, it is unlikely that many students will soon forget the session in which this learning resource is utilized.

   While the film does not emphasize the religious aspects of the lost civilization, neither do the artifacts, uncovered by archeologists since the late 1920s, afford much to go on here—for which reason the film is appropriate to the available data. In any case, a conscientious instructor, using this film to set the context, can supplement what is known about the religious life of the time, perhaps even using commercially available slides for visual support. (See John Frank's very useful set, *Indus Valley Civilization: Bronze Age Technology*, reviewed elsewhere in this section, or, as a distant second-best, selected specimens from the first fifteen slides in the AAR-sponsored set *India— Hinduism*, reviewed in Chapter One.) For those who do not feel competent to advance their own narrations as accompaniment to others' slides, this film may solve most of their problems if the main objective is merely to present in classroom the evidence of Indus Valley archeology in a memorable way.

Portrait of a City
   21 minutes, b/w, 16mm, 1961
   Satyajit Ray
   See Appendix I: Sources of Audiovisual Materials under India, Govt. of . . . , for nearest distribution center of this film.

A "mood" film with no narration in which the camera explores the sights and sounds of Calcutta, India's largest city. The expert hand of director Satyajit Ray is discernible in the richly suggestive juxtaposition of images, the professional style and pacing—an "enrichment" film at its best. For other films of this genre, see *Banaras*, *Gazipur*, and *Indian Village Life . . .* , reviewed elsewhere in this chapter.

Puppeteer
   20 minutes, color, 16mm, 1977
   Sale $220.00, Rental $5.00
   Film Australia—Asian Neighbours series (India)
   Australian Information Service
   Australian Consulate General
   636 Fifth Avenue
   New York, NY 10020

An unusual look at a family from the "Bhat" caste, traditional balladeers of religious and martial poetry. The family lives in a tent in a squatter colony outside the city of Udaipur. The film contrasts the beautiful palaces and Udaipur's historic role as a stronghold of Hindu kingship during the years of the Mughul Empire with the reality of puppet performances in the palaces for tourists and the day-to-day life in the tents. Interviews with the mother and daughter cover child marriage, midwifery, and why they prefer living as resident nomads. The husband, Bansilal, recalls his father's death when he was seven and being told then that as a member of the Bhat caste, puppets would be his life until he dies. Men of the Bhat caste claim Brahmin status, but are reputed to be heavy drinkers, and Bansilal is shown as a habitue of the local bar and grill. While *Puppeteer* is visually excellent and covers aspects of life seldom seen on film, there are some errors in the narration in describing what is seen, and in describing the history of the area. The film may be used effectively to depict how caste traditions are part of the arts, and how an inherited livelihood is changing with the times.

Rabindranath Tagore
  54 minutes, b/w, 16mm, 1961
  Satyajit Ray
  See Appendix I: Sources of Audiovisual Materials under India, Govt. of . . . , for nearest distribution center of this film.

Ray masterfully shows Tagore as he grows from childhood through adult life to old age, and in the process illuminates the great events and intellectual currents which dominate the first half of the twentieth century. Superb footage on Tagore's travels abroad and of his estate in Bengal.

Radha and Krishna as seen through the eyes of the Pahari Painters
  22 minutes, color, 16mm, 1957
  J. Bhownagri
  See Appendix I: Sources of Audiovisual Materials under India, Govt. of . . . , for nearest distribution center of this film. [Note: this film is also available on a rent-free basis from: Public Service Audience Planners, Inc., New York/Chicago/Hollywood. See Appendix I, ibid, for nearest address.]

'A long time ago on the banks of the river Jamuna . . . ,'' so begins this charming evocation of the life of Krishna as a theme of Pahari paintings. Krishna's exploits are somewhat expurgated, and the camera focuses more on the beauty of the painting than on Krishna. Still, this can be a musically and artistically delightful enrichment of any religion course that makes it clear that Krishna's devotees think of his life as something more than a simple story.

Radha's Day: Hindu Family Life
  17 minutes, color, 16mm, 1969
  Sale $180.00, Rental $15.00
  H. Daniel Smith—Image India

Film Marketing Division/Film Rental Library
Syracuse University
1455 East Colvin Street
Syracuse, NY 13210
Also available from UIowa, SyrU, UWash

The camera follows a young unmarried woman in Madras through her daily routine in an urban, middle-class brahman household. Of interest, in addition to caste interactivities through the day, are her devotions to Lakshmi in the home, a visit to a Ganesha shrine with an acolyte shrine to planetary deities, and the decorating of thresholds and doorways. The film is good on ethnographic detail.

Raga
    97 minutes, color, 16mm, 1972
    Sale $1350.00, Rental 125.00
    Howard Worth
    Cornerstone Films
    470 Park Avenue South
    New York, NY 10016

This film focuses on Ravi Shankar and on his deep commitment to his own tradition—especially to the importance of the guru-student relationship. Much of the footage is shot in India, and most of it ties into his religious roots. His devotion to his musical guru and spiritual guru are explicitly shown. There is good footage of the Banaras ghats. Concerts and music lessons predominate in the rest of the film; George Harrison and Yehudi Menuhin make appearances. There is attention to the ephemeral nature of cult-, drug-, and rock-influenced interest in Indian things. The film is visually and musically very entertaining, and can make a good entree to the close relationship of Indian arts and religion.

Raju: A Guide from Rishikesh
    28 minutes, color, 16mm, 1960s
    Sale discontinued, Rental $19.00
    New York University Film Library
    Washington Square
    New York, NY 10003

This film about a nine-year-old tourist guide in this famous Ganges pilgrimage town may give an impression of the lifestyle and mystique of the place even though the camera dwells overlong on the boy. Succeeds in a unique way in revealing religion as a business.

The Sword and the Flute
  24 minutes, color, 16mm, 1959
  Sale $325.00, Rental $30.00
  James Ivory
  Film Images/Radim Films, Inc.
  17 West 60th Street
  New York, NY 10023
  Also available from UCLA, UCt, UIowa, UMinn, UMo, OklaSt, UUtah, WashSt, UWash, UWisc

This is a film montage of Mughal and Rajput miniature paintings focusing on the Mughal period of Indian history, with musical and narrative accompaniment. Most of the scenes depicted in the miniatures dwell on asceticism, love and its allegorical religious implications, and the divine love of Radha and Krishna and, briefly, Shiva and Parvati.

Comments: This is an aesthetically rewarding film; colorful paintings and musical accompaniment by Ali Akbar Khan, Ravi Shankar, T. Vishvanathan, and Chaturlal enhance the setting for this articulate presentation of the allegory and ideals of Bhakti. This film requires careful preparation with attention given to the importance of aesthetics in Indian religion and the frequent allegorical use of the arts. Although it has been in use for many years, it is still one of the most effective film presentations of themes in Bhakti.

Tanjore
  7 minutes, b/w, 16mm
  See Appendix I: Sources of Audiovisual Materials under India, Govt. of . . . , for nearest distribution center of this film.

This film brings out that Tanjore is famous as the birthplace of Tyagaraja and other famous musican saints of South India. Thus, most of this brief film is of annual music concerts honoring Tyagaraja, and the enormous crowds that gather for them. It also contains glimpses of temples and a chariot festival. This film nicely complements what is seen in *A Village in Tanjore: Village Family* (below).

Tantra
  26 minutes, color, 16mm, 1968
  Sale $400.00, Rental $35.00
  Nik Douglas, Robert Fraser, and Mick Jagger
  Cornerstone Films
  470 Park Avenue
  New York, NY 10016

This film includes unusual footage of actual rituals associated with tantra in a montage of scenes intended to give the viewer insight into the stages of awareness and practice of tantra (here called Invocation, Initiation, and Union). Some tantric art is included with footage of tantric practitioners. There is no narrative explanation of what is shown. A discordant musical sound track, trick photography, and footage of dance and pleasing scenery suggest possible interpretations of tantrism.

Temples of Belur and Halebid
14 minutes, b/w, 16mm, 1959
Ezra Mir and Ravi Gabale
See Appendix I: Sources of Audiovisual Materials under India, Govt. of . . . , for nearest distribution center of this film.

A survey of the Hoysala-period temples of northern Karnataka, with close-ups of the incredibly ornate sculptural motifs.

Therayattam
18 minutes, b/w, 16mm, 1959
Sale $150.00, Rental $20.00
K.T. John
Film Images/Radim Films, Inc.
17 West 60th Street
New York, NY 10023

This film attempts through narration to show that dance is an important form of worship. It depicts the elaborate dance of the folk tradition of Kerala, said to be the forebearer of the Kathakali style. In a festival lasting two or three days, the performers portray numbers of gods and goddesses identified with Durga, Kali, Shiva, Ganesha, and Ayyappan. The ceremonial makeup and costuming of the dancers is shown. In spite of the narration, the film does succeed in showing the place of the dance in this folk religion tradition.

Things Seen in Madras
52 minutes, color, 16mm, 1967-68
Sale $795.00, Rental $75.00
Louis Malle—Phantom India
New Yorker Films
16 West 61st Street
New York, NY 10023

Extraordinary footage and narrative which is less objectionable

than Malle's usual. First, a ratha procession through the streets
showing huge crowds and the four-story temple chariot pulled by
human hands. This vivid and sensitive cinematography is followed by
scenes of modern theatre and cinema in Madras. Finally, there is a
quarter-hour in a dance school showing the training, self-sacrifice,
and religious inspiration of the Bharatanatyam.

Village in India: Fifty Miles from Poona
   20 minutes, b/w, 16mm, 1959
   Sale $140.00
   Faili Bilimoria
   National Film Board of Canada
   1251 Avenue of the Americas
   New York, NY 10020
   **Also available from UIowa, BU, UMinn, SyrU, KentSt, OklaSt,
   UTex, UWash**

One of several films available on village India, this is rich in
ethnographic detail. Useful as an enrichment resource in a religion
course for an anthropological approach to the family and community
setting in which faith operates. Filmed in Maharashtra in the late
1950s. Compare *North Indian Village* (above).

A Village in Tanjore: Village Family
   16 minutes, color, 16mm, 1977
   Sale $176.00, Rental $5.00
   Film Australia—Asian Neighbours series (India)
   Australian Information Service
   Australian Consulate General
   636 Fifth Avenue
   New York, NY 10020

No narration interrupts the flow of homely images in this accurately
detailed, ethnographic study of a South Indian village home. The only
words addressed directly to the viewer in English are those spoken at
the very end of the film by the eldest daughter as she reflects upon her
difficulty in fitting prayers into her daily round of activities, and upon
her satisfaction with life in her peaceful village. During the bulk of the
film, the camera simply observes the family inside its rambling,
slightly old-fashioned (but very typical) house in the brahmin sector of
the settlement, and an excursion by the daughter to a nearby city.

It is difficult to gauge how a student unfamiliar with things Indian
will react to the film, so replete with subtle details. It might be utilized
by a resourceful and experienced instructor to initiate discussion on
the place of religion in the home. It would probably require more

than one viewing to do this, however, with tips between screenings from the instructor on what to look for. It is similar to, but more successful than, *Radha's Day*. . . (above); but for best results the two might be used in tandem if the instructional goal is to discern family relationships and to glimpse daily life among middle-class Hindus. Or, if the focus is on household worship, one might consider coupling it, instead, with *How a Hindu Worships: At the Home Shrine* (see Chapter One).

Although this film may be used independently of them, it is itself the third part of a trilogy designed to provide an overview of village life in South India. Part I of the trilogy (*The Village*, 16 minutes) shows morning activities—washing, a sadhu praying, women putting designs on the ground in front of their homes, and Shivaite and Vishnuite devotees applying their respective cosmetic marks. The life of the street reveals various traces of commerce and trade, but an interview with young men brings out problems of staying in the village when jobs are scarce. Part II of the trilogy (*The Village Economy*, 15 minutes) provides an overview of rice farming. Part III, the film under review, presents material with the greatest relevance to courses on Hinduism.

Village Man, City Man
  38 minutes, color, 16mm, 1975
  Sale $140.00, Rental $17.00
  Mira Reym Binford and Michael Camerini
  Department of South Asian Studies
  1242 Van Hise Hall
  University of Wisconsin—Madison
  Madison, WI 53706
  Also available from WashSt, UWash

This film provides an insightful look into the living conditions of a typical village emigree who works in an urban industrial complex, bunks with other men from his region and status, and enjoys only minimum participation in village life when he returns home to his village periodically to visit wife and child and family (whom he supports through his labors). The film can be used to show the ways in which co-religious and other ties preserve a sense of community in the urban world, and how economic necessity keeps many families broken into their rural home life and urban economic components. A condensed version of this film is to be found in *An Indian Worker: From Village to City* (see above).

Viney
  17 minutes, color, 16mm, 1977
  Sale $187.00, Rental $5.00
  Film Australia—Asian Neighbours series (India)
  Australian Information Service
  Australian Consulate General
  636 ɪ ɪfth Avenue
  New York, NY 10020

This film begins with an interview of Viney, a young, well-to-do Hindu housewife, who frankly discusses her arranged marriage (footage includes good home movies of the wedding day), and describes the advantages of living in a joint family, including care of their newborn, shared luxuries (two cars, three-story house, and so forth). Overall, the film provides an uncritical look at the lifestyle of a Hindu family enjoying education and amenities comparable to a Western middle-class family. There is no evidence of worship or other religious practice in the home—a significant point eloquently made by the film. For other films with related interests, see the Topical Index.

Vinoba Bhave: Walking Revolutionary
  39 minutes, color, 16mm, 1970
  Sale $425.00, Rental $22.50
  Pilgrim Films
  International Film Bureau, Inc.
  332 South Michigan Avenue
  Chicago, IL 60604
  Also available from IdahoSt, BU, UMinn, SyrU, UUtah, UWash

Primarily concerned with Bhave's Bhoodan Movement—the attempt to return the land to working peasants—this film gives no evaluation of this controversial program. It ignores Bhave's life and writings but shows his continuity with Gandhi. *Vinoba Bhave—The Man* (20 minutes, b/w, GOI) is a better film but generally not available. May be usefully paired with *Bhoodan Yatra* (see above).

Slides, Filmstrips, Microfiche

Architecture and Sculpture of Orissa: Bhubanesvar and Konarak
100 color slides (2″ x 2″), $100.00 per single set (multiple purchases discounted)
American Committee for South Asian Art Slides Project
ACSAA Slide Project
Department of Art History
Tappan Hall
University of Michigan
Ann Arbor, MI 48109

This set of 100 slides includes pictures of specific temples in the Bhuvaneshwara area: Lingaraja (#1001-1011), Mukteshwara (#1012-1030), Parasurameshwara (#1031-1046), and Rajarani (#1047-1056). The remainder of the set is devoted to the remains of the great Surya temple at Konarak (#1057-1100). Each slide is clearly labeled as to temple illustrated, and the location on the temple of each particular detail, for example, #1067, "Architecture: India, Konarak; Sun Temple, Eastern doorway, right jamb. Detail: Base." These slides were prepared by art historians for art historians; non-specialists will find only a few of the panoramic views and close-ups of some sculptures of relevance to pedagogical needs in a course on Hinduism.

Art and Architecture of Asia
10 slides per set: $3.00 unmounted, $4.00 mounted, $7.50 in glass
Unit cost (per slide): 90¢ unmounted, $1.20 mounted, $1.80 in glass
(Lists sent on request; sets sent on approval)
Budek Films and Slides
1023 Waterman Avenue
East Providence, RI 02914

Budek offers thirty-four sets of slides (ten slides per set) on the art and architecture of Asia. Fifteen of these deal with India. Six provide relevant background for the study of Hinduism. Set 5, Sculpture of the Hindu Dynasties, is comprised of museum pieces. Set 6, The Ellora Caves, includes shots of Hindu caves XV and XXI. Set 7 is Khajuraho. Set 8, Art under the Kushans I, is misnamed and actually contains the Durga temple at Aihole, the Kailashanatha temple at Kanchi, and two temples from Gwalior. Set 9 is Mahabalipuram, and Set 13, Kailasa Temple at Ellora. Overseas Hindu art can be found in the Java and Cambodia sets. Reproduction is good and the color is fair.

NOTE: Regardless of intentions of producers, materials in this section are evaluated according to their usefulness in teaching Hinduism.

Art Slides of India and Nepal
   Sale $1.60 per slide (with quantity discounts); in sets, ca. $1.20 per
   slide.
   Art Slides of India and Nepal
   Inquire: Thomas Donaldson
   3266 Redwood Avenue
   Cleveland Heights, OH 44118

Donaldson offers thousands of slides. Catalogs are currently available covering Buddhist, Islamic, and Mughal art; cave temples;
Chalukyan temples; temples of Orissa, Rajasthan, Gujarat, Maharashtra, Central India, South India; temples and sculptures of Nepal;
and Indian miniature painting. There are no accompanying guides.

Cave Temples of Ellora
   100 color slides (2″ x 2″); $100.00 per set (with discounts for multiple
   purchases)
   American Committee for South Asian Art Slides Project
   ACSAA Slide Project
   Department of Art History
   Tappan Hall
   University of Michigan
   Ann Arbor, MI 48109

A 100-slide set, featuring the Hindu caves hewn from the living rock
at this sixth- to eighth-century site. Emphasis is given to the eighth-
century Kailasha temple dedicated to Shiva, its structural elements and
sculptural details. Slides are clearly identified as to specific structure
and location within them. Many of the slides cater to the interests of art
historians for whom this set is a boon. Non-specialists may find it
problematic to use the slides beyond merely presenting a display of the
extravagant accomplishments of medieval Hindu craftsmen.

Caves
   For detailed information, write:
   Inter Documentation Company
   Poststrasse 14
   6300 Zug, Switzerland

Prepared by Walter M. Spink, this is a microfiche collection of 4,341
photographs and 45 maps and plans of the earliest rock-cut monuments. Mostly Buddhist, with 2,669 from Ajanta, these records form the
basis for the earliest development of Hindu monuments. There are
sections, all available separately, dealing with Hindu monuments.
The collections have short explanatory notes of a few pages. These are

photographic archives, and are not designed for use at a beginning level.

Central Indian Monuments
100 color slides (2″ x 2″); $100.00 per set (with discounts for multiple purchases)
American Committee for South Asian Slides Project
ACSAA Slide Project
Department of Art History
Tappan Hall
University of Michigan
Ann Arbor, MI 48109

This set of 100 slides (numbered 601-700) presents details of sculpture and architectural decoration from a wide range of temples, dating from the sixth through the twelfth centuries. Edited by Michael Meister, the stone temples chosen include: Amrol, Badoh, Barwasagar, Deogarh, Gwalior, Gyraspur, Indor, Kadwah, Khajuraho (636-682), Kuchdon, Mastkheda, Mahua, Naresar, and Umri.

Chalukyan Art
100 color slides (2″ x 2″); $100.00 per set (with discounts for multiple purchases)
American Committee for South Asian Art Slides Project
ACSAA Slide Project
Department of Art History
Tappan Hall
University of Michigan
Ann Arbor, MI 48109

This set of 100 slides (numbered 501-600) represents works within the realm of a single dynasty, monuments which are rock-cut as well as structural creations. Sites and well-known monuments included are: Aihole, Alampur, Badami, Mahakuta, and Pattadakal. A quarter of the slides are interiors or details of interiors. As with other ACSAA sets, the emphasis is on views selected by art historians for use by art historians. The needs of the non-specialist have not been a paramount concern in the preparation of the slides or of the identifying labels.

Fabric of India: Architecture
50-slide set
Sale $50.00

Joan Ferguson
5 Chestnut Hill North
Loudonville, NY 12211

Twelve of the fifty slides in this set deal with Hindu monuments at Mahabalipuram, Madurai, Tanjore, Udaipur, Somnathpur, and Konarak, as well as the tanks at Chidambaram and Tiruchirapalli. Most of the pictures are easily readable, but because they are often fragments and seldom more than one from any single site, it is difficult to get an idea of what is being shown unless one already knows other views. The accompanying brochure has a brief paragraph on each slide providing some useful and some confusing information. The color is washed-out, but the images are clear. These slides are not recommended for independent learning purposes.

Fabric of India: Indian Art—Painting and Sculpture
50-slide set
Sale $50.00
Joan Ferguson
5 Chestnut Hill North
Loudonville, NY 12211

In this set of fifty slides, twenty-one deal with Hindu material: images from Mahabalipuram, Ellora, Somnathpur, Konarak, Chidambaram, Tanjore, Kanchi, and a pair of unspecified bronzes. Many of the slides show only partial images, images out of context or seen from confusing viewing angles, thereby limiting the effectiveness of the picture. The accompanying descriptions are uncritical and often in error. The tone of the writing in the guide is touristy, with questionable points of view expressed and subjective aesthetic judgements made. This set is not recommended for use in independent learning projects. The slide resolution is fair; the color is poor.

Gupta Period
For further information, write:
Inter Documentation Company
Poststrasse 14
6300 Zug, Switzerland

Microfiche collection of 2,257 photographs, plus location maps from numerous sites and museum collections throughout India, that shows the earliest widespread style of Hindu art in monumental materials. This archive was edited by Susan L. Huntington.

Gupta Temples and Sculpture
    100 color slides (2″ x 2″); $100.00 per set (with discounts for
    multiple purchases)
    American Committee for South Asian Art Slides Project
    ACSAA Slide Project
    Department of Art History
    Tappan Hall
    University of Michigan
    Ann Arbor, MI 48109

This is a well-rounded selection of temples and their sculptural
decorations gathered by Dr. Joanna Williams from materials in the
field. Both the best-known monuments such as Deogarh and Nachna
are represented, as well as Udayagiri and Vidisa, and there are a few
slides showing Bhitargaon, Bhimara, Bilsadh, Dah Parbatiya, Eran,
Garhwa, Mandasor, Mukundara, Pipariya, Sanchi, Sarnath, and
Tigawa.

History of Oriental Arts—Hinduism
    300 slides (15 sections of 20 slides each)
    Sale $30.00/section
    Bijuts Shoppon Sa
    Prothman Associates
    650 Thomas Avenue
    Baldwin, NY 11510

In this survey of Oriental art, of special interest to the study of
Hinduism are sets H, I, J, and K. Set H ranges from the Indus Valley to
the Mauryan Dynasty, showing key sculpture and artifacts. Set I is
virtually all Buddhist sculpture. Sets J and K cover from the Kushana
Dynasty (first century A.D.) through the Islamic period (last slide is
labeled 1753 A.D.). While these sets include pieces of Buddhist and
Islamic art, and the overall rationale for their presentation is art-
historical rather than religious, these slides do include many works of
Hindu art of importance and beauty. Overall, these sets offer a good
survey of Oriental art for the informed non-specialist.

Indus Valley Civilization: Bronze Age Technology
    100 color slides, audiocassette, printed description of each slide
    Purchase $16.00 (postpaid), specify audible or silent signal for
    cassette program
    Written, produced, and directed by John Frank for Educational
        Resources Center, New Delhi, and the State Education Depart-
        ment Resources Center, New Delhi, and the State Education

Department of the university of the State of New York, Albany,
1977 Service Center for Teachers of Asian Studies
The Ohio State University
29 Woodruff Avenue
Columbus, OH 43210

The price is certainly right for this set of 100 color slides depicting the Indus Valley sites and artifacts. Included among the visuals are shots of Harappa and Mohenjo-daro today; details of pottery, sculpture, jewelry, and other objects; maps; and imaginative paintings reconstructing how the culture looked in its heyday. Although many religion instructors will not wish to use the programmed presentation prepared by John Frank of the Center for Instructional Resources at SUNY-New Paltz because of its emphasis on technology, others may find it ideal for out-of-class assignment or for independent use in a learning lab. There are some unfortunate lapses in the script as presented by Frank, but on the whole he preserves a sense of mystery about the achievements of the ancient Indus civilization, its still undeciphered script, and the multiple causes of its decline and eventual disappearance. It is unusual to find so many good color shots in one inexpensive collection; the slides alone provide for most instructors more than enough visuals pertinent to their needs for preparing their own, original illustrated presentation on the Indus Valley civilization. Frank himself made a 16mm sound/color film of the sites, *Land of the Indus* (above), but the archeological concerns in it are only incidental. For a more concentrated look at the data on film, see *Pakistan: Mound of the Dead,* also reviewed in this chapter.

Khajuraho
40 slides, color, 1960
Sale $25.00
Walter M. Spink and Deborah Levine
Interbook, Inc.
13 East 16th Street
New York, NY 10003

The set and its accompanying text provide an art history-oriented lecture on the tenth- to twelfth-century Hindu (and Jain) temples at Khajuraho. The text is printed on 5″ by 8″ cards—with a black-and-white enlargement of each slide's image on the reverse of the card bearing the text related to it—making this resource convenient for either independent learning or for lecturing. The text and slides coordinate to give an illustrated discussion of the Hindu temple as a cultural form, and of Khajuraho and its temples in an historical perspective. The text is both scholarly and readable. The grasp of historical and cultural factors is exceptional, even though the main focus is on the history, visual impression, and symbolism of the temples themselves. The discussion and use of sexual imagery on the temples is particularly well handled. However, there is little about how the temples were used in worship, or about ritual practices. The quality of the reproductions is good, although the color is not; however, since most of the images are unpainted stone sculptures, this is no great drawback. This is judged by the panel to be an excellent resource for independent learning purposes.

Kishan Garhi Village. A Generation of Change
   81 b/w, and 100 color slides, 80-page guide
   Sale $70.00
   McKim Marriott
   Interbook, Inc.
   13 East 16th Street
   New York, NY 10003

"Kishan Garhi" is the name applied by anthropologist McKim Marriott to a village in Western Uttar Pradesh, 100 miles from Delhi. The slides in this collection are taken from two field-work periods in the village, the first in 1951-52 (all the black-and-white slides) and the second in 1968-69 (all the color slides). The span of eighteen years suggested the subtitle, *A Generation of Change*; the collection provides the viewer with an opportunity to observe technological, social, and cultural changes over two decades. The section on "Religion" (Hinduism, for the most part), includes only twelve slides, but some forty-three others, such as those under "Caste and Rank," and "A Festival of Rank (Holi)," are relevant. The guide is a versatile and provocative adjunct for independent learning or classroom instruction. There are special sections on women's roles, castes, and occupations. Professor Marriott's contribution is a unique record and an extremely useful one, despite the poor quality of the slides. While not all may agree with his evidence for remarkable changes in Kishan Garhi (which is located in one of the more progressive areas of the subcontinent), the collection affords the student of Hinduism a highly stimulating glimpse of village religion in action. The numbering system on the companion slide sets is confusing.

Kushan Period: Mathura
   For detailed information, write:
   Inter Documentation Company
   Poststrasse 14
   6300 Zug, Switzerland

This is a microfiche archive of 516 photographs of the Kushan art of Mathura, selected by Susan L. Huntington. This is intended primarily for the research scholar, and eventually the resource will record for visual retrieval every useful piece of evidence for studying the tradition.

Mahabalipuram
   76 slides, color
   Sale $40.00
   Walter Spink and Edith Ehrman
   Interbook, Inc.
   13 East 16th Street
   New York, NY 10003

This set of seventy-six slides provides a good selection of general views and sculptural details of the seventh- to eighth-century Pallava Hindu temple complex at Mahabalipuram on the Bay of Bengal, south of Madras city. The final five slides illustrate the continuity of the artistic heritage as taught today in the government art school at Mahabalipuram. The notes are somewhat generalized and uncritical. The color of the slides viewed was slightly washed out.

Nepal
   4 filmstrips. . . . 161 frames, color and sound, 1969, record or cassette
   International Film Bureau, Inc.
   332 South Michigan Avenue
   Chicago, IL 60604

These four filmstrips won the blue ribbon at the American Film Festival in 1969. The first two give a survey of history and geography, while the latter two provide information on the customs of the village people, and on religion and art.

Rajput Miniature Paintings
   100 color slides (2″ x 2″), $100.00 per set (with discounts for multiple purchases)
   American Committee for South Asian Art Slides Project
   ACSAA Slide Project
   Department of Art History
   Tappan Hall
   University of Michigan
   Ann Arbor, MI 48109

This set of 100 slides is comprised entirely of illustrations from a signed manuscript, dated 1648, of the *Bhagavata Purana*. Included in the set, slides #801-900 are depictions of the flood myth, the churning of the ocean, and other myths from the puranic text, including the last days of Krishna. The accompanying text, edited by Suresh Vasant, does not present the *Bhagavata Purana* in its original or in translation; but the sources used are identified, and the subjects of the slides are briefly described in the list. For those who wish to see how Hindu religious texts were illustrated in the traditional way, this is an ideal set. The quality of the reproductions is even better than the usually high standard set by this ACSAA series.

Ramayana Multimedia Unit
   Complete multimedia unit $50.00
   Henry M. Ferguson
   Social Studies Schools Service
   10000 Culver Boulevard
   Culver City, CA 90230

This instructional unit, designed for junior high school students, contains a book synopsis of the *Ramayana* (an undistinguished retelling for young readers), a poster bearing some modernistic line drawings from the book, a wooden cloth-covered box, a cassette tape, and a filmstrip. The filmstrip contains scenes from a Telugu-language movie version of the *Sampoorna Ramayana;* live actors are elaborately costumed as the demons and deities of the epic—a cinema-style presentation which suggests comparison with the *Traditional Theater of South India,* noted below. The cassette is pleasant enough—the Ramayana story is narrated while Chitrababu plays the vina in the background—but it is definitely not geared for adult listeners. While the filmstrip might have some pedagogical uses to college-level instructors in their presentation of the Rama story, the unit is sold only as a package, making the filmstrip fairly expensive for isolated use.

Slide Collection in South Asian Studies
   753 slides, color, 1965
   Sets may be purchased at duplication costs
   Walter M. Spink and Edith Ehrman
   Foreign Area Materials Center
   Center for International Programs and Comparative
   Studies (Henry M. Ferguson, Director)
   The University of the State of New York
   The State Education Department
   Cultural Education Center, Empire State Plaza
   Albany, NY 12230

This is a highly diversified collection of 753 slides that is excellent not only for the study of Hinduism but also for the cultural context of South Asia in general. Part I, Land and People (slides #1-307) includes photos of priests, occupations, landscapes, urban and rural scenes. Part II, Sites and Monuments (slides #308-610) is an alphabetically arranged selection fro Aihole, Ajanta, Barabar Hills, Bhaja, Deogarh, Elephanta, Ellora, Eran, Gwalior, Halebid, Khajuraho, Madura, Mahabalipuram, Mahakut, Mount Abu, Nagral, Sanchi, Somnathpur, and Udayagiri. Part III, Painting (slides #611-753) is devoted to miniatures, about one-third of them relevant to Hinduism—Krishna themes, the Ramayana, Shaiva traditions, etc. The quality of the slides is good. The accompanying catalogue, with black-and-white reproductions of all 753 slides, is a remarkably convenient device for lecture preparation, or independent study, even though it has label information only. Instructors wishing to begin the nucleus for a slide collection might wish to consider acquiring this set as a starter.

South Indian Temples, Sculpture, and Painting
    100 slides (2″ x 2″), $100.00 per set (with discounts for multiple purchases)
    American Committee for South Asian Art Slides Project
    ACSAA Slide Project
    Department of Art History
    Tappan Hall
    University of Michigan
    Ann Arbor, MI 48109

This set of 100 slides (numbered 101-200) covers temples from all over Tamilnadu, as well as selected sites in Karnataka (none from Andra Pradesh or Kerala). There is a balanced selection of images from every major tradition, with some weight given to paintings of the Pallava period. The sites pictured are Chidambaram, Gangaikondacholapuram, Hampi-Vijayanagar, Kanchi, Kodombalur, Kumbakonam, Lepakshi, Madurai, Mahabalipuram, Narttamalai, Panamalai, Pulamangai, Sittannavasal, Shrivilliputtur, Tanjore, Tirukallikunram, Tirukurunkudi, and Tirumalai. While the resource is a welcome addition to the Asian art historian's instructional potential, the non-specialist is left to flounder in regard to how these visuals can best be employed in a classroom setting.

Traditional Theater of South India
    2 filmstrips. . . . 63 frames, color 35mm
    Sale $15.50

Farley Richmond
Olesen
P. O. Box 348
Hollywood, CA 90028

The first filmstrip, "Theater as Ritual," emphasizes that theater in South India is more than just entertainment. Its ritual accompaniments in preparation for performance and in the choice of themes for performance are explained and illustrated. The second strip, "Theater as Entertainment," focuses on the theater craft of masks and makeup and mime. The two strips include references to Kathakali, Yakshagana, and Kuttiyattam styles of performance. Each frame receives about one paragraph of description, and further readings are suggested. The level is college/adult. The sets were made as part of a series for the study of theater craft.

Recordings

The recordings listed here are intended only to suggest some of the available materials; no attempt has been made to note the numerous releases on disc, tape, and cassette reflecting India's rich musical heritage. Consult the most recent Schwann catalogue for stock selections, and refer to Elise Barnett's *Discography of the Art Music of India* (see additional sources in Appendix II).

Ancient and Oriental Music: History of Music in Sound (Vol I)
RCA Records (Education Department)
1133 Avenue of the Americas
New York, NY 10022

Although this 1957 record is not a current issue, it is likely to be found in many college libraries because it was part of the History of Music in Sound series used widely in introductory music courses. Selections on bands 4 to 7 include women's songs from a harvest festival, a weaver's praises to God, and a bhajan (devotional song) sung by a group of villagers outside their temple. There is also a song by the famous saint-musician Tyagaraja, beautifully sung by an unidentified woman musician, and a duet on the shehnai—the instrument popular at weddings and temple ceremonies. The guide, based on the *New Oxford History of Music*, includes musicological notes and photographs of musicians and instruments.

Golden Rain
   Nonesuch Explorer Series H72028
   Nonesuch Records
   665 Fifth Avenue
   New York, NY 10022

Hinduism in Bali has long been separated from its Indian roots, but still plays an important role in music. Ketjak, the startling, staccato Balinese Monkey Chant, highlights performances of the Ramayana in Bali. On Side Two of this recording, the ketjak is suggestive of trance and exorcism as well as of Hanuman's army. The other side has two modern gamelan compositions. The notes are adequate for an introduction to the music and setting of the Monkey Chant. Other recordings of Balinese music in the Nonesuch Explorer Series include: *Gamelan Semar Pegulingan,* recording and notes by Robert E. Brown (H72046); *Music for the Balinese Shadow Play* (music for a Mahabharata shadow-puppet play to placate demons and make dangerous occasions auspicious), recording and notes by Robert E. Brown (H72037); *Music from the Morning of the World,* including a ketjak and a sample of music for a Mahabharata shadow-puppet play, recording and notes by David Lewiston (H72015).

Karnatic Music
   UNESCO Collection—Music of India Album, Record IV
   UNIPUB
   345 Park Avenue South
   New York, NY 10010

This record is useful as an introduction to the music of South India since it utilizes the vina, a stringed instrument extremely popular in South Indian classical performance, accompanied by the typically South Indian mridangam-drum. Moreover, two of the pieces are by one of the most well-known of South Indian composers, Muttuswami Dikshitar—one of the pieces addressed to the Dakshinamurti aspect of Shiva, the other in praise of the goddess Annapurna. Two of the five cuts feature a well-known male vocalist, who sings accompanied by the vina, drum, and drone-like tambura. In all, twelve ragas—all distinctively South Indian—are heard in this recording. The last cut demonstrates the tuning of the vina.

Music of the Dance and Theater of South India
   UNESCO Collection—Music of India Album, Record II
   UNIPUB
   345 Park Avenue South
   New York, NY 10010

This record provides a good introduction to the musical accompaniments of Bharatanatyam and Kathakali, the two major styles of religious art dance in South India, and to the religious poetry that inspires them. The informative notes give approximate musical transcriptions of the themes, but do not provide translations. This record might be used as preparation for an actual performance of Bharatanatyam, or for seeing the film *Balasaraswati,* in which India's great and devoutly religious dancer performs Bharatanatyam. This record will not stand by itself as an introduction to South Indian dance or music.

CHAPTER 3

Hinduism and the West

Films

THE RESULTS OF Hinduism's encounter with the West are manifested in diverse phenomena. Not the least significant among them are the religious and quasi-religious movements which confess allegiance to Hindu norms and/or to personalities inspired by Hindu ideals. Typically, these movements seek to convert Westerners (and Western-oriented Indians) by addressing them in terms compatible with personal backgrounds and motivations—often in the process emphasizing isolated elements within, or steamlining the entirety of the Hindu tradition. A characteristic among many of the current Hindu-inspired movements is concern to share with others their insights, to celebrate their beliefs, to record their histories, by utilizing audiovisual technology. Occasionally, the services of an established documentary filmmaker or professional studio will be co-opted to cater to the concern; sometimes the productions are in-house amateur efforts aimed simply to document specific events or efforts; more often the aims and the execution are quite sophisticated, and are prompted primarily by propagandistic purposes. In any case, what seems to be generated from all this is a corpus of audiovisual materials of growing proportions. Instructors may feel moved to make use of such resources as evidence of Hinduism's continuing vitality or of its steady deterioration, depending on their point of view. What follows is but a partial listing of some of the 16mm sound films which have become available in recent years. The list is *not* exhaustive. Addresses and prices noted are subject to change.

The Avatar: Concept and Example
   This film is reviewed above, on p. 15

Awakening
   30 minutes, color, 16mm, 1975
   Produced by Anthony Hixon
   Film prints available for purchase on a cost-plus basis, videotape version also available on request. (Limited copies available for rental.) Address all inquiries to:

Lewis Buchner
253 Capp Street
San Francisco, CA 94110

This film on Sri Chinmoy's "path" stresses his focus on the integration of meditation with a dynamic outer life. In addition to on-camera interviews with disciples, Sri Chinmoy (b. 1931) also speaks. this film may be used to provide students with a basic introduction to the New York-based guru and to the kind of meditation he teaches, as well as to the spirit that pervades the sixty-or-so Sri Chinmoy centers in the United States and elsewhere. For other resources on Sri Chinmoy, note *Journey's Battle-Victory* and the recording *Music for Meditation* (both reviewed below).

Sophisticated students with powers to discriminate may find it instructive to compare the "path" of Chinmoy with the methodologies espoused in such films as *He Touched Me, Living Yoga,* and *The Spiritual Frontier*, all of which are noted in this chapter.

Ciranjivan
23 minutes, color, 16mm, 1970s
Rental free
The Foundation of Relevation
59 Scott Street
San Francisco, CA 94117

The Foundation of Revelation considers itself a family—of about 200—rather than a movement. This film is a record of relevation (satsang) by Father (Ciranjivan) on Mount Tamalpais, near San Francisco in June 1970. It depicts the spiritual leader and his relationship with devotees—in this case, his "children" or "family." The film has a slight technical defect in that the soundtrack is hard to follow at spots; but that does not significantly detract from its purpose which is to convey the importance to the family-members of being there with the Father. The film is devotional in orientation and tone. See also *Mahamilana*, reviewed below.

Consecration of a Temple
25 minutes, color, 16mm, 1979
Sale $125.00, Rental $17.00
Fred Clothey, Worldview Productions
Department of South Asian Studies
1242 Van Hise Hall
The University of Wisconsin—Madison
Madison, WI 53706

Here is a film which documents the traditional rites of establishing a temple for worship according to Sri-Vaisnava usages which prevail at one of India's most prestigious temples—the Venkateshwara Temple at Tirupati in Andhra Pradesh. The temple being consecrated is, however, in Pittsburgh; it has been built and dedicated to serve traditional Hindus who have made their homes in the Western hemisphere. Artisans were imported from South India to assist in the construction of the imposing ediface; priests were brought from the subcontinent to perform the exacting rituals. This is essentially a filmic record of an event never before so carefully filmed, even in India, let alone in the United States where it is a "first." Instructors will find that this film lends itself for screening in a number of different pedagogical settings. It has been reviewed more fully in Part One, above (page 16).

A Contemporary Guru: Rajnish

This videocassette is reviewed in Part One, above (p. 17).

Evolution of a Yogi
28 minutes, color, 16mm, 1970s
Sale $300.00, Rental $35.00
Elda Hartley—Films for a New Age
Hartley Productions, Inc.
Cat Rock Road
Cos Cob, CT 06807

To a degree, this is a film version of Alpert's *Be Here Now*. In his own disarming words, Ram Dass (né Richard Alpert, 1930) explains his journey from drugs to yoga. The presentation includes a montage of newspaper clippings and photos of Alpert's experiments at Harvard, and some distracting cinematographic effects purporting to show the joyful existence of those who have become his disciples. What is most memorable about the film, however, is Alpert himself; the presentation reveals his charisma as a guru.

The Hare Krishna People
30 minutes, color, 16mm, 1974
Sale $295.00, Rental $30.00
Also available for sale in Super-8 reels, $225.00 and cassettes $260.00
John Griesser and Jean Papert
The Bhaktivedanta Book Trust
3764 Watseka Avenue
Los Angeles, CA 90034

The International Society for Krishna Consciousness produced this attractive and professionally presented film to describe to the outside world the Hare Krishna People—their organization, factories, publishing enterprises, office work for devotional and commercial products, and their communications studios for recording and film-making. It shows devotees in characteristic activities in Los Angeles, New York, London, India, Mexico, and at the "New Vrindavana" Farm in West Virginia. The underlying spiritual tone is enhanced by the musical background of the typical Hare Krishna chants, rhythms and bells, and by the continuous presence of artwork depicting Krishna. The film ends with an American Krishna devotee commenting on the late Swami Prabhupada's rendering of the *Bhagavad Gita*, and a shot of Prabhupada himself in the Hare Krishna dance with other devotees at a temple.

For a more up-to-date presentation of approximately the same material, and one available in an easy-to-use format of slides and audio-cassette (hence, recommended either for classroom use or for independent study purposes), see *ISKCON: New Cult or Old Culture* (slides section, below).

Hatha Yoga Darshana: The Yoga Point of View
   30 minutes, color, 16mm, 1970s
   Sale $440.00, Rental $50.00
   Jim Kaspar
   Kaspar Productions, Inc.
   P.O. Box 60
   Newton Center, MA 02159

This film is technically oriented, dealing with one person exhibiting and explaining physical yoga. The practitioner (Haven O'More) explicates the spiritual significance along with the health advantages of yoga. The two aspects—the technical and the philosophical—are fused into an absorbing presentation. The advanced level of approach suggests that this is a film which will have greatest impact on students already familiar to some degree with things Hindu and Indian, or to those who are particularly interested in yoga.

He Touched Me
   45 minutes, color, Super-8mm
   Inquire: Kripalu Yoga Retreat
   Box 120
   Summit Station, PA 17979

While there is a great deal of walking around and shots of the beautiful scenery at the Kripalu Yoga Retreat, there is also presentation of the basic structure and nature of this group, including focus on its founder Yogi Amrit Desai and his guru, Swami Shri Kripalvanandaji. This Super-8-format film gives a considerable amount of information, devotional in tone, about the yoga practiced for the inner-self. It makes an interesting comparison with other groups, such as the followers of Satchidananda whose karma yoga is meditation in action (see, for example, the film *Living Yoga*, reviewed below), or the Hare Krishna group at "New Vrindavana" where karma yoga is work for Krishna (see, for example, *The Spiritual Frontier*, also noted below).

Journey's Battle-Victory
  15 minutes, color, 16mm, 1977
  Produced by Silver Journey Productions
  (Film prints available for purchase on a cost-plus basis; videotape version on request. Limited copies available for rental.)
  Inquire: Lewis Buchner
  253 Capp Street
  San Francisco, CA 94110

Sri Chinmoy (b. 1931) stresses that meditation should free one to act more creatively and dynamically in everyday life. He is certainly living testimony to his doctrine. He has composed many thousands of "poems" (843 in one twenty-four-hour period); over 250 books quote "verbatim" his counsels (including those delivered in the prestigious Dag Hammarskjöld Lecture Series at the United Nations); since 1974 he has painted or sketched over 100,000 of what he calls his "fountain art" (16,031 created in one twenty-four-hour period); he is a composer and performing musician as well (see review of recording *Music for Meditation . . .* , below). This film, then, is a remarkable documentation of his extraordinary powers as a painter, and records the creative process as he works on a 12' by 25' acrylic painting on canvas. Very little is said by way of narration, beyond a few words by Chinmoy at the commencement; for the rest, the soundtrack features Chinmoy's music played by him on the bowed esraj, or on an alto flute. This is an eloquent film to illustrate Chinmoy's teaching regarding the relationship between meditation and creative accomplishment. See also the film *Awakening*, reviewed above.

Krishnamurti: A Dialogue with Huston Smith
  63 minutes, color, 16mm, 1971
  Sale $600.00, Rental $60.00

School of Theology, Claremont
Blaisdell Institute
143 East 10th Street
Claremont, CA 91711

Many people regard Krishnamurti (b. 1895) as an articulate expression and exemplar of an imaginative and sensitive blending of Western philosophy and Indian wisdom. This interview, filmed in 1968, elicits from him reflections on freedom, authority, relationships, the ideal and nature of love. Additional films of lectures by J. Krishnamurti are available for sale or rent from Indiana University AV.

Living Yoga
    20 minutes, color, 16mm, 1960s
    Sale $275.00, Rental $30.00
    Integral Yoga Institute
    Satchidananda Ashram, P.O. Box 108
    Pomfret, CT 06259
    or:
    Hartley Productions, Inc.
    Cat Rock Road
    Cos Cob, CT 06807

Focusing on Swami Satchidananda (b. 1914), the film treats four paths, or yogas, separate from one another yet much like the spokes of a wheel—all leading to the hub, the oneness. Hatha is the way of the body; raja, the way of the mind (meditation); karma is the way of service (meditation in action); and bhakti, the way of the heart ("you just love"). In this presentation, one should note that jnana, the way of the intellect, is significantly absent—indeed, in a final scene Satchidananda tells his devotees to cut off the head as love comes from the heart and not from the head. While it could be argued that correct knowledge, or jnana, is implicit (as wisdom) in the other four, it can also be held that it is a traditionally separate yoga and deserves treatment as such. Still, the film purports to treat Satchidananda's views, not philosophical Hinduism as such. For other films on yoga, consult the Topical Index.

Mahamilana
    27 minutes, color, 16mm, 1970s
    Available for loan only
    The Foundation of Revelation
    59 Scott Street
    San Francisco, CA 94117

Much can be learned about The Foundation of Revelation from this film, one which might usefully be paired for screening with *Ciranjivan*, reviewed above. In this, one views the arrival in California from Bengal of the immediate family of the founder, or Father, of The Foundation of Revelation group. Their separation from Ciranjivan had been long and filled with tribulations, and the shots of the reunion are frankly sentimental as well as spontaneously joyous. Their greeting by members of the Foundation is a good example of the closeness expressed. At times folksy and homey, the ingenuousness and warmth of this family reunion has the grace and charm of an insider's view, not unlike that of any home movie of a family reunion.

Maharishi Mahesh: Jet-Age Yogi
 28 minutes, color, 1960s
 Inquire: New York University Film Library
 Washington Square
 New York, N. Y. 10003

This film opens as the leader of the Spiritual Regeneration Movement arrives in a helicopter at Rishikesh, where awaiting him are the Beatles, the Rolling Stones, the Beach Boys, and assorted disciples, theatrical and otherwise. This mid-1960s film is an honest attempt to explore Maharishi Mahesh as a contemporary phenomenon of India and of the West. In a personal interview during part of the film, direct questions concerning his method and clientele are more or less responded to.

New Age Communities: The Search for Utopia
 40 minutes, color, 16mm, 1970s
 Sale $400.00, Rental $45.00
 Elda Hartley
 Hartley Productions, Inc.
 Cat Rock Road
 Cos Cob, CT 06807

"New Age" alternate lifestyles are presented through five communal settlements: "Twin Oaks" near Richmond, Virginia, with no dominant ideology; "Koinonia" near Baltimore, religiously oriented but undoctrinaire; "The Farm" at Summertown, Tennessee, eclectically based upon Hindu-Buddhist thought and led by Stephen Gaskin; "Ananda Cooperative Village" near Nevada City, California, founded by Swami Kriyananda (né Donald Walters), disciple of Paramahamsa Yogananda; and "Findhorn" on the northeast coast of Scotland, also spiritual but undoctrinaire. Informative and especially valuable for comparison of "The Farm" and the "Ananda Cooperative Village" as similar—but by no means the same—in spiritual approach and lifestyle.

Non-Violence—Mahatma Ghandi and Martin Luther King: The Teacher and the Pupil

This film is reviewed in Chapter Two, above (page 91). For other treatments of Gandhi, see the Topical Index.

Raga

This film profile of Ravi Shankar, containing scenes from concerts the masterful sitar player gave in the United States, is reviewed in Chapter Two, above (page 168).

Sathya Sai Baba: His Life is His Message

The "Miracle Man" of South India (b.1926) has a small (but growing) number of followers in this country. This is only one of several available films depicting aspects of his career and ministry, and is reviewed in Chapter One, above (page 47).

Spark of Life
   24 minutes, color, 16mm, (n.d.)
   Sale $295.00, Rental $30.00
   (Also available in Super-8 reels and cassettes, as well as in
   videocassettes)
   The International Society for Krishna Consciousness
   The Bhaktivedanta Book Trust
   3764 Watseka Avenue
   Los Angeles, CA 90034

Available prints of this film were all in use at the time this volume went to press. A description of the film's contents was kindly provided by the producer-distributor, quoted here in lieu of a first-hand review:

"Conversations between two college students explore theories on the nature of life as proposed by modern scientists and by the 5,000-year-old *Bhagavad-Gita*. One student, relying on the things he is learning in a biology course, maintains the scientific thought regarding life as a material phenomenon, with memory and personality being the results of genes and a series of complex chemical processes. His friend, who has been studying the *Gita*, argues that scientists theorize about what they don't know on the basis of what little they do know; he maintains that within the body is an antimaterial particle which is the source of conscious life and the essence of personality. After much discussion, the first student finally concedes that even modern science cannot fully and satisfactorily explain what and where life is, and accepts the possibility of his friend's contentions. They go on to discuss death, explained by the *Gita* as the antimaterial particle leaving the body, and the individuality and quality of all living things, in accordance with the equality of individual antimaterial particles. A basic introduction to Indian thought as laid down in the *Bhagavad-Gita*."

The Spiritual Frontier
   27 minutes, color, 16mm, 1976
   Sale $295.00, Rental $30.00
   (Also available for sale in Super-8 reels, $225.00 and cassettes, $260.00)
   John Griesser and Jean Papert
   The Bhaktivedanta Book Trust
   3764 Watseka Avenue
   Los Angeles, CA 90034

The spiritual frontier is the way of life exemplified by the Hare Krishna people at their commune, "New Vrindavana" in West Virginia. The initial sequence shows the temple where the founder of the International Society of Krishna Consciousness, Swami Prabhupada (b. 1896), lived for twelve years. Then in 1965, the narrator explains, in response to his guru's order, he came to New York City with the Krishna mantra, where he "urged his disciples to found an ideal community" which would be a "spiritual frontier." New Vrindavana is now "one of the largest religious communities, covering some thousand acres in the foothills of West Virginia." There are shots of the building of new temples, cabins, and workshops in progress, and of classes, dancing, and singing. The viewer with a background knowledge of Hinduism will see evidence of the transplanting of a romanticized India, the modeling of the devotees on the example of the guru, and of the firm commitment of the devotees to a highly structured, well-organized religious group.

Sunseed
   87 minutes, color, 16mm, 1971
   Rental $90.00

Frederick Cohn and Ralph Harper Silver
Cornerstone Films
470 Park Avenue South
New York, NY 10016

This is a popular and ambitious film on "New Age" groups or movements. It spends a great deal of time on the late Murshid Samuel Lewis, and varying amounts of footage on Lama Anagarika Govinda, Swami Satchidananda, Ram Dass, Swami Muktananda, Yogi Bhajan, among others in India and the United States. It is an atmospheric film providing more mood and message than objective information, with a considerable degree of sentimentality—but it is useful for enrichment purposes.

Swami Karunananda: From Wallaroo, Australia

The teachings of Swami Sivananda have influenced many Westerners, including an Australian who, renouncing his former life and family ties, went to live at the Sivananda Ashram in Rishikesh. This film is reviewed in Chapter One, above (page 51).

Swami Shyam

This film is reviewed in Chapter One, above (page 51).

Time of the Saviour
   24 minutes, color, 16mm, 1973
   Sale $350.00, Rental $50.00
   Jim Kaspar
   Kasper Productions, Inc.
   P.O. Box 60
   Newton Center, MA 02159

This film is an examination of Guru Maharaj Ji's (b.1957) Divine Light Mission, a critical analysis of the psychology of such movements and their effect upon Americans. The film uses the Divine Light Mission as a case study, not a target in itself, and raises questions rather than provides answers. Even though the nature and phrasing of the questions have an obvious negative undertone, the issues raised make the film useful for students who have only modest background derived from a study of Hinduism to approach such movements in America with some sophistication.

The Universal Flame
    28 minutes, color, 16mm, 1975
    Free loan only
    Hartley Productions in collaboration with The Theosophical Society
    Inquire: Modern Talking Picture Service
    2323 New Hyde Park Road
    New Hyde Park, NY 11040
    Booking: St. Petersburg, Florida
    (tele: 913-541-6661)
    Also available from UIll

The Theosophical Society, with its world headquarters in Madras and its American headquarters in Wheaton, Illinois, was one of the earliest groups dedicated to infusing Western culture with Eastern wisdom. The Theosophical Society was originally formed in New York City by Helena Petrovna Blavatsky, and this film was produced in 1975 to mark the centenary of that founding. In the film the remarkable personality of Mme. Blavatsky is treated not so much as what she represented in her own time but more in terms of her resonances with the spiritual aspirations of a "New Age," an age in which there is renewed quest for convincing answers to man's eternal questions. Not the least attractive feature about this professionally produced film is its availability on free loan.

Slides

[Note: The leader here is clearly The Bhaktivedanta Book Trust. Slides are occasionally available from other groups. See Appendix II: Sources for Additional Information.]

Death and Rebirth in Vedic India
    49 slides, programmed audiocassette, script
    Sale only $49.00
    The Bhaktivedanta Book Trust
    3764 Watseka Avenue
    Los Angeles, CA 90034

The term "Vedic" in the title does not pertain to ancient Aryan tribal customs in the subcontinent. It is, in fact, a usage adopted by members of the ISKCON movement in their efforts to legitimize their ideology—based on the sixteenth- and seventeenth-century teachings of the post-Caitanya Goswamis of Bengal—by associating it with "ancient" Indic doctrines. Without a thorough knowledge of the Vedic texts and traditional Hinduism, the script will be misleading and simplistic. For example: "The soul evolves step by step through eight million species of life before it reaches the human form" (slide #13); "At age fifty, a man customarily leaves his wife and family in care of his eldest son and accepts sannyasa, the renounced order of life . . . one simply practices spiritual activities until he passes away" (slide #29); "According to Vedic tradition, corpses should be burned" (slide #36). These are all best understood as statements of faith by members of ISKCON. The visuals contain scenes photographed in India interspersed with paintings produced by ISKCON studios. Slides #33–43 depict steps in a cremation rite; a resourceful instructor could gainfully use those by providing a more sophisticated and ethnographically telling commentary than the prepared script offers. A more advanced and concentrated treatment of the subject is found in the videocassette *Death and Rebirth In Hinduism* (see Chapter One).

F.A.T.E.—Bengali Religious Art Comes to the West
   54 slides, programmed audiocassette and script, 1977
   Sale only $54.00
   The Bhaktivedanta Book Trust
   3764 Watseka Avenue
   Los Angeles, CA 90034

F.A.T.E. is an acronym for "First American Theistic Exhibit," a permanent exhibition by ISKCON in Los Angeles of diorama settings that illustrate Hindu themes favored by the Krishna-Consciousness Movement, and featuring life-size figures, advanced lighting effects, and electronically programmed music. This tape-slide presentation chronicles the genesis of the project to its recent installation for public display. The narrator comments that a combination of Eastern craftsmanship and philosophy with Western technology has resulted in the creation of ". . . an intriguing new art form in America"— although some critics might argue whether it is on the one hand, new, and on the other hand, art. Yet whatever else it is, it is spectacular! Among the finished, life-size dioramas seen depicted here: Bhaktivedantaswamy Prabhupada studying the *Gita*; the famous scene of Krishna counseling Arjuna on the battlefield; the "Age of Man" tour de force; Vishnu recumbent; Krishna with the gopis; and Caitanya singing in ecstasy.

ISKCON: New Cult or Ancient Culture
   69 slides, programmed audiocassette and script, 1979
   Sale only $69.00

The Bhaktivedanta Book Trust
3764 Watseka Avenue
Los Angeles, CA 90034

This is perhaps the best package available in attractive, handy-to-use, and relatively inexpensive format which presents the International Society for Krishna Consciousness in a way that is consistent with the cult members' own attitudes about their past history, present vitality, and future expectations. It is eloquent testimony, indeed, and may be utilized by classroom students and by independent learners either as an *emic* or as an *etic* model for study. Recommended especially for situations in which a learning goal is the influence of Hinduism in the West, this tape-slide production supercedes the earlier film, *The Hare Krishna People* (above).

Recordings

During the past few years, when Hindu-related sects have proliferated in the West, many of the movements began producing recordings on tapes for dissemination among believers, as well as for placing their respective teachings before the public. This is one of the cheapest methods contemporary technology presents for distribution of lectures, liturgies, celebrations, and interviews. It is not surprising, then, that there are now available vast quantities of such recorded materials. They present a significant potential for teaching and research. Because of an almost normative lack of scholarly authentication and notes, a persistently haphazard and usually underground distribution arrangement—to say nothing of their sheer quantity—no systematic attempt has been made to catalogue them in this volume. What follows is merely a suggestive sampling. Those who wish to employ such materials in class will wish to consult the Appendices for addresses to write for further information, and to follow other avenues of locating sources known to them. Simply because an item is not listed here implies no commentary on its usefulness for instructional purposes.

Maharishi Mahesh Yogi: Deep Meditation
World Pacific Records, WP 1420, 1962
A Richard Bok Production

Side One contains an "inaugural lecture by His Holiness Maharishi Mahesh Yogi," delivered at Guild Hall in Cambridge, England, on July 11, 1960. Here the guru says he has come out of the Himalayas because "something must be done" to "satisfy the needs of man"; to regenerate the head and heart of man by "meditation." In order to "look within," he proposes a technique to get to man's "transcendental being, a state of pure, absolute consciousness." He protests that the technique is "not new"; only the assurance that it is "easy" is a message new to man. His down-to-earth message, in ordinary language, reveals the charm that was to attract to him so many followers in the months and years which followed.

Side Two is a quietly authoritative address on "Healing Powers of Deep Meditation," delivered the year before on May 2, 1959 in Hollywood Congregational Church. Both of these recordings have at least a historical interest inasmuch as they come from a period near the beginning of his first "ten-year missionary program" in the West.

The Mother Reading the Mother
  4 LP records, price $27.00
  Matagiri/Sri Aurobindo Center, Inc.
  Mount Tremper, NY 12457

In 1926, Sri Aurobindo Ghosh (1872–1950) founded an Ashram in Pondicherry, along the shores of the Bay of Bengal in South India. Soon after, he was joined there by a gifted French woman, Mira Richard (1877–1973). Through the many years of their close collaboration as partners in an unparalleled spiritual adventure, both wrote, both kept journals, he as spiritual head of the community, she as its administrative "Mother." This is an album of four LP records of "The Mother" reading from some of Aurobindo's better known essays and from some of her own works. In addition, the recordings present two passages of The Mother's own music composed for electronic organ. This is a recording prized—not only by the international community of followers who honor Sri Aurobindo and The Mother as prophets of a New Age when a higher consciousness prevails—but also as a rare recording of the beloved visionary and mystic remembered, simply, as The Mother.

Music for Meditation: Sri Chinmoy
  Folkways Records, FR 8935
  Produced by Neil Vineburg; pamphlet notes by Nemi
  Folkways Records
  43 West 61st Street
  New York, NY 10023

Sri Chinmoy (b. 1931) was reared in the Sri Aurobindo Ashram in Pondicherry, South India. He arrived in the United States in 1964 and soon attracted—and has retained—a strong following in the Eastern United States, where since the late 1960s he has frequently sponsored meditation at the United Nations Headquarters and at major American universities. A few years ago he gained wide publicity from his prodigious painting (10,000 paintings in one month). Recently, over 100 of his followers completed the 1979 New York Marathon. This album features the vigorous mystic playing a bowed musical instrument (esraj), reciting English "poems" of his composition, singing several Bengali devotional songs, and enunciating a fifteen second "aum." The record jacket cautions: "This album should be listened to at a soft volume during meditation."

The Radha-Krishna Temple London
   Apple Records, SKAO 3376
   Produced by George Harrison
   Apple Records
   1700 Broadway
   New York, NY 10019

This record clearly calculates its pitch to a commercial audience who will be "turned on" by the gently rocking, romantic renditions of "Krishna Consciousness" chants. The first cut on Side One is a pleasant, and very contemporary, mannered paean to "Govinda," accompanied by electric guitar, which builds to an orchestrated climax. The second cut is a relatively brief, sweetly sung and chastely executed male vocal selection addressing the spiritual master ("Shri Guru-vashtakam"). This is followed by a set of two more traditional bhajana-type songs. The jacket notes indicate these are typical of what is sung in ISKCON temples while the Lord is offered foodstuffs; its professionally polished rendering is, however, more reminiscent of Indian movie music than of naive temple devotional music. The side ends with an extended (3½ minutes) celebration of the Hare Krishna Mantra; an electronically amplified bass and several studio effects add to the excitement of this section.

Side Two presents a four-minute singing of the first three verses of the *Ishopanishad* which sounds—to the uninitiated ear, at least—more like the Beatles than the bhaktas. The main selection on this side is an unpretentious performance of an eighteenth-century song, attributed to Govinda Dasa; it is accompanied by harmonium and clappers. The production winds up with the mantra "Govinda Jaya Jaya," performed in a way presumably typical of vocally trained Krishna Consciousness devotees.

The Rhythm of Shiva
   2 stereo audiocassettes, packaged, 1978
   The Summit Lighthouse for Church Universal and Triumphant
   Box A
   Malibu, CA 90265

This attractively packaged set of two stereophonically recorded audiocassettes contains eight bhajanas (devotional hymns) in Sanskrit addressed to Shiva, interspersed with four meditational messages by "Guru Ma"—the Messenger Elizabeth Clare Prophet who spearheads a movement known as The Summit Lighthouse/Church Universal and Triumphant. Consequently, the presentation is an uneven mixture of traditional bhakti celebration in antiphonal musical form and of inspired utterances by a young American woman—whose prophecies are claimed to be the very words dictated to her by the Lord Shiva Himself (and whose body is believed to be the Divine Dancer's holy instrument). The cassettes are accompanied by two slip sheets pertaining, respectively, to the two components of this package.

The bhajanas may prove useful as an introduction to the genre. These could be used also to set a "mood" in the classroom when an emphasis on Shiva bhakti is an objective. A printed phonetic guide to the words in the bhajanas is provided—as is also a translation into English—for those who may wish to learn the hymns in praise of Shiva. While the selections are presumably traditional stotras (verses) set to music, there is no indication of source; nor is the male song leader identified. Evidently, the mixed male-female antiphonal chorus is comprised of devotees of S.A.I. Foundation ("Spiritual Advancement of the Individual"), to whom appreciation is expressed for making possible the publication of the tapes.

As for the four meditations by Messenger Elizabeth Clare Prophet, the "World Mother"—43, 17, 11, and 37 minutes long respectively—these will be of greatest interest (aside from her own immediate followers) to those involved in the study of personality cults or concerned with the analysis of the eclecticism of contemporary Asian-related cults in America. It should be noted that the passages quoted on the enclosed sheet, attributed to "Lord Shiva" and "Ishwara," are excerpts from this lady's addresses here recorded.

The Sounds of Yoga Vedanta

This record is reviewed in Chapter One, above (page 71).

Temple Music and Chants with Sri Swami Rama
   1973 (reissued 1977), record or cassette, $5.95
   Himalayan International Institute
   RD 1 – Box 88
   Honesdale, PA 18431

Side One includes an Upanishadic passage rendered as a prayer ("asate ma sadgamaya—Lead me from untruth to Truth"); praises sung by the disciples to the guru; and the chanting of "Hare Krishna, Hare Rama" and other simple phrases by a chorus made up largely of Westerners. Side Two includes an adequately sung poem composed by Kabir, the sixteenth-century Hindu poet-saint, and a ten-minute performance by Satish Kumar on sitar.

The notes include fanciful etymologies used by the sect as a didactic device (e.g., "People think that the word guru means teacher, but that is not true. The word guru is composed of two words, gu and ru. Gu means darkness and ru means light"; or "Krishna is a Sanskrit word meaning the center of attraction"; etc.). The record jacket and other publications of the group claim that Sri Swami Rama ". . . at the age of twenty-four became Shankaracharya (a Hindu position somewhat analogous to pope [sic])."

I

Sources of Audio-visual Materials

IN ALL ENTRIES noted in the foregoing volume, addresses given pertain to purchase orders. Those same sources often also rent the same materials—although it should be noted only rarely do slides, film-strips, videocassettes, and recordings circulate on a rental basis. In this appendix are brought together all the sources indicated in the reviews. Attention is called first, however, to other regional, non-commercial sources for film rentals to which inquiries may be addressed for availability of specific titles, rental fees, and other information.

A. Non-Commercial Sources

The very first place to which any instructor or independent learning group should turn for film rentals are the local film rental sources. Often, these provide services more quickly and at lower cost than commercial distributors. These are of three varieties—regional university film-rental libraries, local libraries with audiovisual departments serving community needs, and federally funded South Asia studies centers with varying facilities for assistance.

1. University Film Rental Libraries

The university film rental libraries have been consulted extensively for this series, and they have copies of many of the films reviewed in this guide. These libraries are listed by state, with a guide to the abbreviations used in the present work, following the Directory of Producers and Distributors.

See also: *University and College Film Collections: A Directory,* compiled by Indiana University Audio-Visual Center and Consortium of University Film Centers (New York: Educational Film Library Association, 43 W. 61st St. NY 10023, 1974), 76pp., $7.00. This offers a state-by-state listing of 415 film collections, giving the size of the collection, addresses, and availability for rental. Collections listed range in size from under 100 films to over 10,000.

[Note: Film libraries seldom have more than one print of a film. Potential users should make sure the film will be available on the days desired. The Syracuse University Film Library catalogue states that priority is assigned to orders as received, and that requests for the following academic year start arriving at Syracuse in March. Always plan to preview a film before using it, often difficult when rental sources ship films to arrive on the day of screening.]

2. Public Libraries
Public libraries are frequently a good, inexpensive source for films about India. Policies vary; some libraries discourage borrowers from using their films for classroom purposes, yet welcome their use by civic and religious groups as well as by independent learners.

3. South Asia Centers
For the years 1977-1979, there were eight designated South Asia Centers to be financed by the U.S. Office of Education under Title IV of the National Defense Education Act. Part of their grants must be spent for off-campus education; in some cases, that means providing information and audio-visual materials for the study of South Asia. The Centers designated, to which inquiries may be addressed, were:

California:
South Asian Language and Area Studies Center
University of California - Berkeley
Berkeley, CA 94720

Illinois:
South Asian Language and Area Center
University of Chicago
Chicago, IL 60637

New York:
South Asian Center
School of International Affairs
Columbia University
New York, NY 10027

Pennsylvania:
South Asian Language and Area Studies Center
University of Pennsylvania
Philadelphia, PA 19174

Texas:
Center for South Asia
University of Texas
Austin, TX 78712

Virginia:
South Asian Studies Center
University of Virginia
Charlottesville, VA 22903

Washington:
South Asian Language and Area Studies Center
University of Washington
Seattle, WA 98195

Wisconsin:
Center for South Asian Studies
University of Wisconsin - Madison
Madison, WI 53706

B. Producers and Distribution Sources Utilized in this Survey

(For additional sources to contact for audiovisual resources and other learning materials not reviewed in this volume, see Appendix II: Sources for Additional Information, below.)

Academic Support Center Film
   Library
The University of Missouri -
   Columbia
505 East Stewart Road
Columbia, MO 65211

ACSAA Slide Project
Department of Art History
Tappan Hall
University of Michigan
Ann Arbor, MI 48109

Apple Records
1700 Broadway
New York, NY 10019

Argus Communications
7440 Natchez Avenue
Niles, IL 60648

Art Slides of India and Nepal
Attention: Thomas Donaldson
3266 Redwood Avenue
Cleveland Heights, OH 44118

Asian Studies Education Project
New York University
Washington Square, 735 East
   Building
New York, NY 10003

Atlantis Productions, Inc.
1252 La Granada Drive
Thousand Oaks, CA 91360
(tele: 805-495-2790)

Audio Brandon Films, Inc.
34 MacQuesten Parkway South
Mt. Vernon, NY 10550
(tele: 914-664-5051)

Audio-Visual Center
Indiana University
Bloomington, IN 47401

Australian Information Service
Australian Consulate General
636 Fifth Avenue
New York, NY 10020
(tele: 212-245-4000)

B.F.A. Educational Media
2211 Michigan Avenue, P.O. Box
   1795
Santa Monica, CA 90406

Benchmark Films, Inc.
145 Scarborough Road
Briarcliff Manor, NY 10510
(tele: 914-762-3838)

James Beveridge Associates
c/o Edna and Friends, Inc. - Room 503
18 West 45th Street
New York, NY 10036
(tele: 212-869-8419)

The Bhaktivedanta Book Trust
Audio-Visuals Division
3764 Watseka Avenue
Los Angeles, CA 90034
(tele: 213-555-4455)

Blaisdell Institute
143 East 10th Street
Claremont, CA 91911

Boite à Musique
133 Boulevard Raspail
Paris VI, France

Lewis Buchner
253 Capp Street
San Francisco, CA 94110
(tele: 415-861-4146)

Budek Films and Slides
1023 Waterman Avenue
East Providence, RI 02914

Center for Arts
Wesleyan University
Middletown, CT 06457

Center for Instructional Resources
State University College at New Paltz
New Paltz, NY 12561

Center for International Programs
and Comparative Studies
(Henry Ferguson, Director)
New York State Education
Department
The University of the State of
New York
Cultural Education Center
Empire State Plaza
Albany, NY 12230

Centron Educational Films
1621 Ninth Street, Box 687
Lawrence, KA 66044

Cinema 5 - 16mm
595 Madison Avenue
New York, NY 10022

Fred Clothey
Department of Religious Studies
2604 Cathedral of Learning
University of Pittsburgh
Pittsburgh, PA 15260

Contemporary/McGraw-Hill Films
1221 Avenue of the Americas
New York, NY 10020

Cornerstone Films
470 Park Avenue South
New York, NY 10016
(tele: 212-684-5910)
or Attention: Fred Cohen
811 18th Street
Boulder, CO 80302

Coronet Instructional Films
65 East South Water Street
Chicago, IL 60601

Marie Joy Curtiss
103 Burlington Drive
Manlius, NY 13104

Department of South Asian Studies
Distribution Office
1242 Van Hise Hall
1220 Linden Avenue
University of Wisconsin - Madison
Madison, WI 53706

Encyclopedia Britannica
Educational Corporation
425 North Michigan Avenue
Chicago, IL 60611

Extension Media Center
University of California - Berkeley
Berkeley, CA 94720

Joan Ferguson
5 Chestnut Hill North
Loundonville, NY 12211

Film Images/Radim Films, Inc.
17 West 60th Street
New York, NY 10023
(tele: 212-279-6653)

Film Marketing Division/Film
Rental Library
(see Syracuse University)

Focus International, Inc.
505 West End Avenue
New York, NY 10024
(tele: 212-799-0491)

Folkways Records
43 West 61st Street
New York, NY 10023

The Foundation of Revelation
59 Scott Street
San Francisco, CA 94117

Hartley Productions, Inc.
Cat Rock Road
Cos Cob, CT 06807
(tele: 203-869-9633)

Himalayan International Institute
R.D. 1 - Box 88
Honesdale, PA 18431

Ideal Picture Co.
34 MacQuesten Parkway South
Mt. Vernon, NY 10550
(tele: 914-664-5051)

India, Govt. of . . .
(See also Public Service
Audience Planners, Inc.)
   Northeast & Midwest:
      Consulate General of India
      3 East 64th Street
      New York, NY 10021

   South:
      Information Service of India
      2107 Massachusetts Avenue, NW
      Washington, DC 20008

   West:
      Consulate General of India
      215 Market Street
      San Francisco, CA 94105

Integral Yoga Institute
Satchidananda Ashram
P.O. Box 108
Pomfret, CT 06259

Inter Documentation Company
Poststrasse 14
6300 Zug, Switzerland

Interbook, Inc.
13 East 16th Street
New York, NY 10003
(tele: 212-964-4263)

International Film Bureau, Inc.
332 South Michigan Avenue
Chicago, IL 60604

International Film Foundation, Inc.
475 Fifth Avenue, Suite 916
New York, NY 10017
(tele: 212-685-4998)

Kaspar Productions, Inc.
P.O. Box 60
Newton Center, MA 02159

Kripalu Yoga Retreat
Box 120
Summit Station, PA 17979

Learning Corporation of America
1350 Avenue of the Americas
New York, NY 10019
(tele: 212-397-9330)

Matagiri/Sri Aurobindo Ashram,
   Inc.
Mount Tremper, NY 12457

McGraw-Hill Films
(see Contemporary/McGraw-Hill)

Media Guild
118 South Acacia
Solona Beach, CA 92075

Modern Talking Picture Service
2323 New Hyde Park Road
New Hyde Park, NY 11040
(booking: St. Petersburg, FL
   tel: 813-541-6661)

National Film Board of Canada
1251 Avenue of the Americas
New York, NY 10020
(tele: 212-586-2400)

Navin Kumar, Inc.
967 Madison Ave.
New York, NY 10021

New Line Cinema Corporation
853 Broadway, 16th Floor
New York, NY 10003
(tele: 212-674-7460)

New York University Asian Studies
   Education Project
(see: Asian Studies Education
   Project)

New York University Film Library
Washington Square, 41 Press Annex
New York, NY 10003

New Yorker Films
16 West 61st Street
New York, NY 10023
(tele: 212-247-6110)

Nonesuch Records
665 Fifth Avenue
New York, NY 10022
(tele: 212-484-8030)

Olesen
P.O. Box 348
Hollywood, CA 90028

Peters International, Inc.
619 West 54th Street
New York, NY 10019

Phoenix Films, Inc.
470 Park Avenue South
New York, NY 10016
(tele: 212-684-5910)

Pictura Films Distribution Corp.
118 8th Avenue
New York, NY 10011
(tele: 212-691-1730)

Prothman Associates
650 Thomas Avenue
Baldwin, NY 11510
(tele: 516-223-1420)

Public Service Audience
    Planners, Inc.
    East:
        1 Rockefeller Plaza
        New York, NY 10020

    Midwest:
        645 North Michigan Avenue
        Chicago, IL 60611

    West:
        6290 Sunset Boulevard
        Hollywood, CA 90028

Pyramid Films
Box 1048
Santa Monica, CA 90406

Quest Films
The Theosophical Society in
    America
P.O. Box 270
Wheaton, IL 60187

Radim Films/Film Images
1034 Lake Street
Oak Park, IL 60301

RCA Records (Educational
    Department)
1133 Avenue of the Americas

New York, NY 10022
(tele: 212-598-5900)

Record and Tape Sales Corporation
95 Christopher Street
New York, NY 10014

Sathya Sai Baba Center & Bookstore
7911 Willoughby Avenue
Los Angeles, CA 90046
(tele: 213-656-9373)

Scholarly Audio-Visuals, Inc.
5 Beekman Street
New York, NY 10038
(tele: 212-571-7520)

Service Center for Teachers of
    Asian Studies
The Ohio State University
29 Woodruff Avenue
Columbus, OH 43210

Social Studies Schools Service
10000 Culver Boulevard
Culver City, CA 90230

The Summit Lighthouse for Church
    Universal and Triumphant
Box A
Malibu, CA 90265

Syracuse University Film Marketing
    Division/Film Rental Library
1455 East Colvin Street
Syracuse, NY 13210

Teletape Associates
2728 Durant Avenue
Berkeley, CA 94704

Threshold Films
2025 North Highland Avenue
Hollywood, CA 90068

Time-Life Multimedia
100 Eisenhower Drive,
    Box 644
Paramus, NJ 07652
(tele: 201-843-4545)

UNIPUB
345 Park Avenue South

New York, NY 10010
(tele: 212-686-4707)

The University of Missouri -
  Columbia
(see Academic Support Center
  Film Library)

Visual Education Service
The Divinity School, Yale University
409 Prospect Street
New Haven, CT 06511

Xerox Films
245 Long Hill Road
Middletown, CT 06457

University Film Libraries

Key to "Also Available From" institutional sources mentioned within
text and listed alphabetically *by order of state.*

Arizona:

ArizSt   -Arizona State
           Central Arizona Film
             Coop.
           Audiovisual Center
           Tempe, AZ 85281
           602/965-5073

UAriz   -University of Arizona
           Bureau of Audio
           Visual Services
           Tucson, AZ 85706
           602/884-3282

California:

UCB   -University of
             California/Berkeley
           Extension Media Center
           2223 Fulton Street
           Berkeley, CA 94720
           415/642-0460

UCLA   -University of California/
             Los Angeles
           Instructional Media
             Library
           Royce Hall 8
           405 Hilgard Ave.
           Los Angeles, CA 90024
           213/825-0755

Colorado:

UCol   -University of Colorado
           Educational Media
             Center
           348 Stadium Bldg.
           Boulder, CO 80302
           303/492-2530

Connecticut:

UCt   -University of Con-
             necticut
           Center for Inst. Media &
             Technology
           Storrs, CT 06268
           203/486-2530

Florida:

FlaSt   -Florida State University
           Instructional Stupport
           Center Film Library
           030 Seminole Dining
             Hall
           Tallahassee, FL 32306
           904/644-2820

USoFla   -University of South
             Florida
           Film Library
           4202 Fowler Avenue
           Tampa, FL 33620
           813/974-2874

Idaho:

Boise   -Boise State University
           Educational Media
             Services
           1910 Col. Blvd.
           Boise, ID 83720
           208/385-3289

IdahoSt   -Idaho State University
           Audio Visual Services
           Campus Box 8064
           Pocatello, ID 83209
           208/236-3212

Illinois:

NoIll -Northern Illinois
        University
        Media Distribution Dept.
        De Kalb, IL 60115
        815/753-0171

SoIll -Southern Illinois
        University
        Learning Resources
        Services
        Carbondale, IL 62901
        618/453-2258

UIll   -University of Illinois
        Visual Aids Service
        1325 South Oak Street
        Champaign, IL 61820
        217/333-1360

Indiana:

IndSt -Indiana State University
        Audio Visual Center
        Stalker Hall
        Terre Haute, IN 47807
        812/232-6311

IndU   -Indiana University
        Audio Visual Center
        Bloomington, IN 47401
        812/337-2103

Purdue -Purdue University
        Audio Visual Center
        Stewart Center
        West Lafayette, IN 47907
        317/749-6188

Iowa:

IowaSt -Iowa State University
        Media Resource Center
        121 Pearson Hall
        Ames, IA 50010
        515/249-8022

Kansas:

UKans -South Asia Program
        University of Kansas
        Manhattan, KA 66502

Maine:

UMe   -University of Maine

Instructional Systems
Center
16 Shibles Hall
Orono, ME 04473
207/581-7541

Massachusetts:

BU   -Boston University
        Krasker Memorial Film
        Library
        765 Commonwealth
        Avenue
        Boston, MA 02215
        617/353-3272

Michigan:

UMich -University of Mighigan
        Audio Visual Education
        Center
        416 Fourth Street
        Ann Arbor, MI 48103
        313/764-5360

Minnesota:

UMinn -University of Minnesota
        Audio Visual Library
        Services
        3300 University Ave., Se
        Minneapolis, MN 55414
        612/373-3810

Missouri:

UMo   -University of Missouri
        Academic Support
        Center
        505 E. Stewart Rd.
        Columbia, MO 65211
        314/882-3601

Nebraska:

UNeb   -University of Nebraska/
        Lincoln
        Instructional Media
        Center
        Nebraska Hall 421
        Lincoln, NE 68588
        402/472-1911

New York:

NYU   New York University
       Audio-Visual Center

Washington Square
New York, NY 10003

SyrU   -Syracuse University
Film Rental Center
1455 E. Colvin St.
Syracuse, NY 13210
315/479-6631

North Carolina:
UNoCar   -University of North
Carolina
Bureau of Audio Visual
Education
P.O. Box 2228
Chapel Hill, NC 27514
919/933-1108

Ohio:
KentSt   -Kent State University
Audio Visual Services
330 Library Bldg.
Kent, OH 44242
216/672-3456

Oklahoma:
OklaSt   -Oklahoma State
University
A-V Center
Stillwater, OK 74074
405/624-7212

Pennsylvania:
PennSt   -The Pennsylvania State
University
Audio Visual Services
Special Services Bldg.
University Park, PA
16802
814/865-6314

South Carolina:
USoCar   -University of South
Carolina
Audio Visual Services
Columbia, SC 29208
803/777-2858

Tennessee:
UTenn   -University of Tennessee
Teaching Materials
Center

R-61 Communications
Knoxville, TN 37916
615/974-3236

Texas:
UTex   -University of Texas
at Austin
General Libraries
Film Library
Box W
Austin, TX 78712
512/471-3573

Utah:
BYU   -Brigham Young
University
Educational Media
Center
290 Herald R. Clark
Building
Provo, UT 84602
801/374-1211
x3456

UUtah   -University of Utah
Educational Media
Center
207 Milton Bennion Hall
Salt Lake City, UT 84112
801/581-6112

Washington:
WashSt   -Washington State
University
Instructional Media
Services
Pullman, WA 99164
509/335-4535

UWash   -University of
Washington/Seattle
Instructional Media
Services
23 Kane Hall DG-10
Seattle, WA 98195
206/543-9909

Wisconsin:
UWisc   -University of Wisconsin/
Madison
Bureau of Audio-Visual

Instruction
1327 University Avenue
Madison, WI 53706
608/262-1644

Wyoming:
UWy   University of Wyoming
Audio Visual Services

Box 3273 University
  Station
Room 14 Knight Hall
Laramie, WY 82071
307/766-3184

Sources for Additional Information

EXPERIENCED USERS of audio-visual resources to assist the learning process realize that the search for suitable materials is continuous. This appendix is designed to provide leads for those who, despite inexperience, wish to reach out beyond what this volume offers in order to find new and additional resources.

A. Reference Lists

1. Filmographies and Film Lists

An Annotated List of the Audio-visual Resources at South Asia Media Center, Media Center, Kansas State University, edited by Anvita Abbi. Manhattan, KS: South Asia Media Center, Kansas State University, 1976, 24 pp. This guide includes films, video, slides, filmstrips, records, and tapes. It does not give information on sources for these materials, and the annotations are sketchy. Since the collection was accumulated with the primary purpose of supplying the high schools and junior colleges of Kansas, the level of the films is generally below adult learning needs. This resource bank is primarily of regional interest.

Asia Through Film, edited by Jo Ann Hymes. Ann Arbor, MI: Project on Asian Studies in Education, University of Michigan, 1976, 64 pp. $3.50. This guide omits in this printing the major portion of films on South Asia. It includes films on China, Japan, and Southeast Asia, but does not index China and Japan under religion. The annotations are clearly written, but the evaluations are uncritical. The films are available for rent through the University of Michigan Audio-Visual Education Center.

Audio-visual Resource Guide, edited by Nick Abrams. New York: Friendship Press, 1972, 478 pp. $8.95. (Subtitle: "How to Find the Best in Films, Filmstrips, Slides, Records, Tapes, Picture Sets, and Other Audio-Visuals.") For schools, churches, and community organizations, this is one guide that does pay special attention to religion. One subsection of the guide is devoted to religions of the Third World.

Ethnographic Film, by Karl G. Heider. Austin, TX: University of Texas Press, 1976, 166 pp. $8.95. This book, which lists about fifty films with annotations, systematically outlines the history of films, the economics of filmmaking, and the uses of ethnographic films in the classroom. It is written in a clear, discursive style and provides helpful insights for showing, watching, or making films about another culture.

Film and the Humanities, New York: Rockefeller Foundation, 1977. 1133 Avenue of the Americas, NY 10036. Free. Representatives in the field write about the use of films in the humanities. Includes a bibliography of books and articles and a reference guide for locating and evaluating films.

A Filmography of the Third World, compiled by Helen W. Cyr. Metuchen, NJ: Scarecrow Press, 1976, 319 pp. $12.50. This ambitious guide lists films distributed or available in the United States and Canada. Sources and complete cinematographic data are given along with one-sentence annotations. Some University Film Rental Library collections are also listed. There are over 100 films on India, and more on Southeast Asia.

Films for Anthropology Teaching, compiled by Karl G. Heider. Washington, DC: American Anthropological Association, 1977 (3rd revised edition), 187 pp. $5.00. This guide provides an alphabetical annotated listing of about 780 films, indexed by geographic area (over fourty films on South Asia) and by topic, including sections on "ritual" and "life-cycle." It includes descriptions of several films from the 1930s. Source data is given for all films.

Films for Study of India, compiled by Mira Binford. New Delhi: Educational Resources Center, 1971. Free from CENTER FOR INTERNATIONAL PROGRAMS AND COMPARATIVE STUDIES, New York Education Department, Cultural Education Center, Empire State Plaza, Albany, NY 12230. Mira Binford, the filmmaker for the University of Wisconsin South Asia Films, has compiled this guide to films available in India, giving clear descriptions and helpful comments.

Guide to Films on Asia. New York: The Asia Society (725 Park Avenue, NY 10021). This guide is the by-product of a film festival and review, held in December 1975, on films about Asia. Over 100 films are listed with annotations and evaluations. Further information sources are also given.

Guide to Indian Dance, by Judy Van Zile. Providence, RI: Brown University Press, 1972. $3.00. This guide includes a partially annotated listing of over twenty films, and a list of recordings.

India on Film, compiled by Uma de Cunha. New Delhi: Educational Resources Center, 1973, 80 pp. Free from CENTER FOR INTERNATIONAL PROGRAMS AND COMPARATIVE STUDIES, New York State Education Department, Cultural Education Center, Empire State Plaza, Albany, NY 12230. This is an annotated listing of films made and distributed in India, with a final ten pages on films by non-Indian filmmakers. Over 300 films are listed with clear notes, and recommended films are marked with an asterisk. Religion and philosophy is one of the categories covered. Many of the films may be obtained through Government of India offices in the United States.

Learning About India: An Annotated Guide for Nonspecialists, edited by Barbara J. Harrison. Albany, NY: New York State Education Department, 1977. $3.95. Also available from the above CENTER FOR INTERNATIONAL PROGRAMS, this guide includes listings of over 100 films with annotations, as well as records, slides, and other audio-visual aids for teaching about India. The guide provides a useful compendium of current books and institutional resources for the study of India.

National Information Center for Educational Media (NICEM). University of Southern California, University Park, Los Angeles, CA 90007. NICEM catalogues provide the most comprehensive lists of educational films, video, and filmstrips. They are indexed under a variety of headings, including Philosophy and Religion. However, the user is always advised to check with the distributors of films directly to see if they are really available since many films get into the catalogue without being successfully or long distributed.

South Asia Film Collection. Seattle, WA: South Asia Resource Center, University of Washington, 1976. This is an annotated listing of films available through the University of Washington film library, giving dates, format, and length of films, but not other sources for rent or purchase. The list includes eighteen films on Hinduism; a good selection, but the descriptions are generally uncritical.

2. Slide Guides

A Guide to Slides on Asia. New York: The Asia Society, n.d. $1.30. A nine-page mimeographed listing of sources for buying slides, indicating general geographical areas in Asia handled by respective purveyors. No critical evaluations; not very useful.

Slide Buyers Guide, edited by Nancy Delaurier. New York: College Art Association (3rd revised edition), 1976. Available from the College Art Association of America, 16 East 52nd Street, New York, NY 10022, this work lists the major suppliers of art slides, and gives general information on their prices, catalogues, business practices, and the quality of their slides. There is a subject index referring the reader to the suppliers of slides. Under geographical areas, twenty-nine dealers are given for slides on India (seven are overseas). The introduction gives helpful information on evaluating, buying, and preserving slides, as well as on color fidelity and retention of various reproduction techniques.

3. Discographies and a Partial List of Addresses for Additional Recordings

A Discography of the Art Music of India, compiled by Elise B. Barnett. Ann Arbor, MI: The Society for Ethnomusicology, 1975, 54 pp. $4.00. This lists 315 records of Indian art music released prior to January 1, 1973. The artists, instruments, and ragas (if any) are given along with source and record number. The annotations indicate reviews in the *Journal for Ethnomusicology*. The records are listed alphabetically by distributor.

Folkways Records: Mail Order Catalogue. Write to Folkways Records, 43 West 61st Street, New York, NY 10023. This ten-page mail order catalogue of nearly 2,000 titles includes over twenty-five recordings of Indian music, including Indian art music as well as recordings of the sound of Hindu sectarian movements in the West. Folkways' printed guides supplied with some records are generally much more helpful than the notes found on most record jackets. Many recordings go back to the early 1950s and have been continually available.

The Full Circle Archive provides a cooperative distribution and lending service to members, to whom tapes and videocassettes may be rented for $1 plus postage. Currently, their catalogue ($2, which can be applied to the $12 membership fee) lists about 500 items, ranging from *A Conversation with Joseph Campbell* to *Zen: The Eternal Now— Alan Watts*. A number of contemporary American spiritual groups are represented, including Gurus Yogi Bhajan, Swami Amar Jyoti, Ramamurti Mishra, Yogeshwara Muni, Muktananda, Sivanada Radha, and Venkatesananda. All transactions are on an honor system, with the assumption that those wanting their own copies will buy them from the commercial distributors or owners. [Note: this operation recently changed hands and in November 1978, suspended operations "temporarily" in order to undergo quality-control development and reassessment; potential users are urged to check the current status of the archive before placing orders.] Write: P.O. Box 4370, Boulder, CO 80306.

Journal of Ethnomusicology. Published by the Society for Ethnomusicology, 201 South Main Street, Room 513, Ann Arbor, MI 48108, the *Journal* reviews records and films of musical performance, and is a primary source for information concerning Hindu religious music.

Nonesuch Records (665 Fifth Avenue, New York, NY 10022). Especially in its Explorer series, Nonesuch Records represent a rich resource for recordings of authentic Hindu religious music. Other Asian religious traditions are also available. Check your local record shops before writing; Nonesuch has a good distribution network.

Oriental Music: A Selected Discography, compiled by International Institute for Comparative Music Studies and Documentation in Berlin (Jacques Brunet, editor), 1971, 100 pp. $3.00. Available from New York State Center for International Programs (see next section.) This discography includes about fifty titles of Indian music, as well as music of the Middle East, North Africa, Central Asia, Southeast Asia, East Asia. Each listing gives the title, sources, instruments used by the performers, and occasional descriptive notes.

Pacifica Audio Programs & Pacifica Tape Library (5316 Venice Boulevard, Los Angeles, CA 90019). Selected interview and other public information format programs from the Pacifica radio network stations are available for purchase. Of over 15,000 programs in the archive, approximately one-sixth have been announced in annotated catalogues. The two most recent are available for $1 each and list over 1,000 programs, including a number on India, modern religious movements, and world religions. Both the library and the catalogues are expanding and this is likely to be an increasingly significant source of radio (especially educational radio) programs. Tapes are for sale on either reel or cassette, and average $12 for a one-hour program.

Peters International, Inc. (619 West 54th Street, New York, NY 10019) is the sole U.S. distributor for the leading Indian recording companies, and European companies as well. Records may be ordered directly from their *Illustrated Catalog of Imported Indian Recordings* (price of catalogue $1). This currently lists over 200 recordings, including both film tunes and classical recordings. The guide includes a number of albums classified by language.

B. Inquiries May Be Addressed to the Following Individuals and Institutions
[Note: This list is *by no means* exhaustive.]

1. For further information on the cultural background of Hinduism:

American Committee for South Asian Art, Newsletter *Editor, Professor Holly Hutchens, The School of the Art Institute of Chicago, Columbus Drive and Jackson Boulevard, Chicago, IL 60603*

"ACSAA" is a non-profit, voluntary society of scholars who specialize in South or Southeast Asian art—as collectors, art historians, connoisseurs, or as museologists—all dedicated to the encouragement and advancement of the study of the arts in those areas, and to the communication and sharing of knowledge among scholars and other persons interested in those arts. Panels are sponsored annually by ACSAA at both the Association for Asian Studies and the College Art Association. A *Newsletter* is published twice a year from the above address (back issues available). Listing new visual resources in the field, exhibitions, and traveling artists programs, it is available to members free of charge. Membership is by payment of annual dues. For information of schedules, contact Ms. Janice Dundon, Treasurer, ACSAA, Division of History of Art, The Ohio State University, Columbus, OH 43210. ACSAA has sponsored production of almost two dozen sets of color slides in collaboration with Professor Walter Spink of the Department of Art History, The University of Michigan— many of which are reviewed elsewhere in this volume. ACSAA has also undertaken an "Outreach Operation," by which it seeks to address the needs of learners in American schools and colleges, churches and civic groups, through production of visual resources pertaining to South Asian art.

The Asia Society, 725 Park Avenue, New York, NY 10021.
This is a multifaceted organization worth getting to know (member-ships in various categories available). The India Council is charged with various educational and dissemination projects; the Performing Arts Council assists in booking performances of Asian artists, and also has films and videotapes of actual performances available for purchase or rental; the Society for Asian Music provides discographic informa-tion. Unfortunately, The Asia Society's occasional lists of films on Asia are seldom comprehensive or up-to-date; nevertheless, they are helpful so far as they go.

Asianists' Teaching Network, c/o Lee A. Makela, Department of History, Cleveland State University, Cleveland, OH 44115.
This is a recently formed organization dedicated to the encouragement of professional development and teaching excellence through im-proved communication, and the sharing of instructional resources and strategies among college and university teachers in Asian studies. A *Newsletter* has been initiated, copies of which are sent to subscribers at $2.00. (See Service Center for Teachers of Asian Studies, below.)

Association for Asian Studies, Lane Hall, University of Michigan, Ann Arbor, MI 48109.
The AAS quarterly *Newsletter* occasionally notes new teaching resources, but the coverage is both irregular and uneven. Membership fees on application.

Atlantis Productions, Inc., 1252 La Granada Drive, Thousand Oaks, CA 91360.
Many who have used the film *Asian Earth* will be interested to learn that twenty years later, *Asian Earth: A New Generation,* is scheduled for release. The same filmmaker returned to the original village to document the change experienced by a farm family in the course of a generation. Other new films of peripheral interest to users of this volume include *Jhalda, in the Gangetic Plain,* as well as one surveying Eastern religions.

Broadcasting Foundation of America, 52 Vanderbilt Avenue, New York, NY 10017.
The Broadcasting Foundation of America supplies radio programs from foreign stations, and has a number of programs from India, including at least five of religious music with one half-hour program on the Vedas.

Center for International Programs and Comparative Studies (Henry M. Ferguson, Director), The University of the State of New York, the State Education Department, Cultural Education Center, Empire State Plaza, Albany, NY 12230.
This office has taken a leading role for the past fifteen years or more in the production and dissemination of learning resources for studying foreign areas, including India. Currently available are films, film-strips, slides, slide sets, audiotapes, and other learning packages

which this office either sells directly or has produced for sale through other outlets. New materials are constantly being added to their inventory, including printed matter. Request to be placed on their mailing list for announcements.

Marie Joy Curtiss, 103 Burlington Drive, Manlius, NY 13104.
Specializes in ethnomusicology, with particular interest in the musical traditions of India. Tapes of Indian classical music, three films on music education in India and other topics; almost 1,000 slides of musical instruments, performers, and related subjects.

Educational Film Library Association, 43 West 61st Street, New York, NY 10023.
The Educational Film Library Association is a major clearing house of information on educational films. It sponsors an annual American Film Festival at which selected new educational films, including ethnographic films and films on religion, are screened and judged. Members receive a subscription to EFLA's journal, which lists new releases.

Educational Resources Center, P.O. Box 3554, New Delhi, 110024, India.
An outreach arm of the CENTER FOR INTERNATIONAL PROGRAMS AND COMPARATIVE STUDIES of the State Education of the University of the State of New York (see above), this center has produced two catalogues of Indian films and continually serves to assist in the making of films, slides, filmstrips, and other learning packages focused on India. Address inquiries to the Albany address, above.

Encyclopedia Ethnographica, American Archive, The Pennsylvania State University, Audio-visual Services, 17 Willard Building, University Park, PA 16802.
This is a film-lending archive primarily of silent films of ethnographic importance. Films generally come with a guide or monograph and many are under five minutes in length. Film rental prices average about $1.00 per minute.

Joan Ferguson, 5 Chestnut Hill North, Loudonville, NY 12211.
A veteran professional who has provided educators with learning resources on India for well over a decade, Mrs. Ferguson can provide information regarding slides and slide sets formerly available through the now-defunct Interculture Associates, as well as in regard to newer materials.

IND-US, Inc., P.O. Box 56, East Glastonbury, CT 06025.
Book and other print materials, formerly distributed by Interculture Associates, are now handled through this newly created outlet. Direct inquiries to attention of Kamala Srinivasan.

International Association of the Vrindaban Research Institute, School of Oriental and African Studies, University of London, Malet Street, London WC 1 E 7HP, England.
Slides, other photographic materials, explanatory cassettes, and other publications relating to sects having their focal point in Vrindaban,

with special interest in modern Vaishnava Hinduism of North India.

Service Center for Teachers of Asian Studies (F. R. Buchanan, Director), The Ohio State University, 29 West Woodruff Avenue, Columbus, OH 43210.

Among the several services provided is publication of a quarterly guide to instructional materials, *Focus* (subscriptions $2 per year). It includes announcements of and advertisements for new materials, chiefly for secondary schools use. (See Asianists' Teaching Network, listed above.)

Social Studies Schools Service, 10000 Culver Boulevard, Culver City, CA 90230.

Handles all filmstrips and multimedia units formerly distributed by the now-defunct Interculture Associates; also specializes in resources useful for secondary schools teachers dealing with units on India.

The Society for Folk Arts Preservation (Evelyn Stern, Director), 308 East 79th Street, New York, NY 10021

This fledgling organization already boasts a collection of thousands of slides of various folk arts, including a large number from India. It aims to document folk art and folk religion through visual means including film and video.

Society for Visual Anthropology, c/o Professor Jay Ruby, Temple University, Philadelphia, PA 19122.

This organization may be helpful in providing information about anthropological materials in films useful for background studies for Asian religions, and for news of current film projects. Each year the society hosts a film festival at which new documentary films are screened and judged.

Unipub, 345 Park Avenue South, New York, NY 10010.

This is the official U.S. distributor for many UN and UN-sponsored materials, including the UNESCO series of books and records, as well as a number of slide sets on the art of the non-Western world. Some of these materials have been reviewed elsewhere in this volume.

2. *Additional sources of audiovisual materials and information on the study of Hinduism in America may be obtained by contacting such organizations as the following:*

Aum Publications, P.O. Box 32433, Jamaica, NY 11431.

Books, mainly the verbatim transcriptions of addresses and reflections of Sri Chinmoy (b. 1931), an English-speaking personality based in the Queens area of New York and not to be confused with Swami Chindmayananda, an English-speaking personality based mainly in India. Two films and a record of Sri Chinmoy are reviewed elsewhere in this volume.

The Bhaktivedanta Book Trust, Audio-visuals Division, 3764 Watseka Ave., Los Angeles, CA 90034.

Books, pamphlets, films, videocassettes, audiocassettes, slides, filmstrips, photos, posters and other materials relating to the International Society for Krishna Consciousness (ISKCON, also popularly known as "The Hare Krishna Movement"). New and notably professional audiovisual resources being produced regularly by this energetic cadre of devotees, all celebrating and aiming to disseminate the tenets of their faith.

Big Sur Recordings, 2015 Bridgeway, Sausalito, CA 94965.
Send for list of available recordings.

Blue Mountain Center of Meditation, Box 381, Berkeley, CA 94701.
Offers series of tapes and cassettes relating to Eknath Easwaran's methods of meditation.

Chinmaya Mission, Sandeepany West, 835 Main Street, Napa, CA 94558.
Tapes and cassettes available. Swami Chinmayananda, an English-speaking personality based mainly in India, is not to be confused with Sri Chinmoy, an English-speaking personality based in New York's Queen's area.

Hanuman Storehouse, P.O. Box 1569, Santa Cruz, CA 95061.
Books, photos, gift items "sadhana articles," and other paraphernalia related to devotion to Rama, Krishna, Anandamayi Ma, Baba Hari Dass, Ramana Maharshi, Hanuman Prasad Poddar, Sri Ramakrishna, Swami Ram Dass, and others.

Himalayan International Institute, RD 1 - Box 88, Honesdale, PA 18431.
Books on yoga, meditation, psychotherapy, cookery, and other subjects, with a growing inventory of audiocassettes and other materials.

Integral Yoga Institute, Satchidananda Ashram, P.O. Box 108, Pomfret, CT 06259.
The followers of the charismatic Satchidananda, who opened the original Woodstock Festival, have already made one film in collaboration with Hartley Productions, *Living Yoga* (q.v., Chapter Three), and disseminate other materials relating to their guru's views.

New Age Communications, P.O. Box 3284, Monterey, CA 83840 (Attention: Richard Hooper).
For tapes and cassettes of radio broadcasts and related communications by a wide spectrum of personalities representing "New Age" consciousness.

New American Religions Project, c/o Professor Frederick W. Blackwell, Department of Foreign Languages and Literatures, Washington State University, Pullman, WA 99164.
This represents an effort to study systematically various "New Age" religious movements, with focus primarily upon groups which center around a guru, whether traditional or innovative. Professor Blackwell proposes to produce a comprehensive descriptive analysis of groups with bibliographies and pertinent audiovisual lists, as a major output of his projected effort. Currently, he maintains a listing

of these guru-oriented groups and organizations, copies of which are available for $2.

New Dimensions Foundation, 267 State Street, San Francisco, CA 94114.

For tapes and cassettes of radio broadcasts and related communications by a wide spectrum of personalities representing "New Age" consciousness.

Sanatana Dharma Foundation, 3100 White Sulphur Springs, St. Lehena, CA 94574.

Tapes and cassettes on meditation methods recommended by Yogeshwar Muni.

San Francisco Service Distributing Company, 2438 16th Avenue, San Francisco, CA 94116.

Handles disc and cassette recordings of Sri Chinmoy and others.

Sathya Sai Baba Center & Bookstore, 7911 Willoughby Avenue, Los Angeles, CA 90046.

Books, records, films and slides, cassette tapes, photographs, and other matter related to the South Indian personality-cult figure, Sathya Sai Baba (b. 1926).

Sri Sathya Sai Baba Book Center of America, P.O. Box 278, Tustin, CA 92680.

Books, records, films, slides, cassette tapes, photographs, and other matter related to the South Indian personality-cult figure Sathya Sai Baba (b. 1926).

The Summit Lighthouse, Box A, Malibu, CA 90265.

Tapes, publicity folders, educational programs, and the like, focused on the teachings of Messenger Elizabeth Clare Prophet, Ascending Masters, and the Church Universal and Triumphant.

The Theosophical Society in America, P.O. Box 270, Wheaton, IL 60187.

Provides information on Quest Films, Quest Books, and other materials related to The Theosophical Society.

Selected List of Filmmakers, Narrators, Series

(Unless otherwise noted, all entries are films or videocassettes)

Abbas, Yavar	Maharishi Mahesh: Jet-Age Yogi / Raju: Guide from Rishikesh / Swami Karunananda: From Wallaroo, Australia
Altars of the World (series)	(See: Ayres, Lew)
Australia, Film	Padma, South Indian Dancer / Swami Shyam / A Village in Tanjore: Village Family
Ayres, Lew	Hinduism: Wheel of Karma / Holy Men of India: The Sadhus
B.B.C. - Open University	Avatar: Concept and Example (in collaboration with Robert A. McDermott) / The Wages of Action: Religion in a Hindu Village (in collaboration with the University of Wisconsin South Asian Studies Department) / (See also Eyre, Ronald, below)
Beveridge, James	Bhismallah Khan / Four Religions (Part I and Part II) / Music of North India: Four Indian Musicians (Bhimsen Joshi, Pandit Jasraj, Vijay Rao, Amjid Ali Khan)
Binford, Mira Reym and Camerini, Michael	Banaras / Four Holy Men: Renunciation in Hindu Society / An Indian Pilgrimage: Kashi / An Indian Pilgrimage: Ramdevra / An Indian Worker: From Village to City / Village Man, City Man / Wedding of the Goddess
Clothey, Fred	Consecration of a Temple / Pankuni Uttaram: Festival of Marriage and Fertility / Skanda-Sasti: A Festival of Conquest / Yakam: A Fire Ritual . . .
Contemporary South Asian Film Series	(See: Binford/Camerini)
Elder, Joseph	(See: B.B.C. - Open University; also, Binford/Camerini)
Exploring the Religions of South Asia (series)	(See: Knipe, David)

Eyre, Ronald	Hinduism: 330 Million Gods
Film Australia	(See: Australia)
Films for a New Age (series)	(See: Hartley, Elda)
Hanneman, Yvonne	Murugan
Hartley, Elda	Bali Today with Margaret Mead / Evolution of a Yogi / Hinduism and the Song of God / India and the Infinite: The Soul of a People / New Age Communities: The Search for Utopia
Hitchcock, John and Patricia	Gurkha Country / Himalayan Shaman: Northern Nepal / Himalayan Shaman: Southern Nepal / North Indian Village
Image India: The Hindu Way (series)	(See: Smith, H. Daniel)
India, Gov't. of	Bhoodan Yatra / Cave Temples—Hindu / Festival Time / Holy Himalayas / Invitation to an Indian Wedding / Kailash at Ellora / Khajuraho / Konarak / Kucchipudi—Part One / Madhubani Painters / Portrait of a City / Rabindranath Tagore / Radha and Krishna . . . / Tanjore / Temples of Belur and Halebid
India Called Them (series)	(See: Abbas, Yavar)
ISKCON	The Bhagavad Gita Illustrated (slides) / Death and Rebirth in Vedic India (slides) / F.A.T.E.: Bengali Religious Art Comes to the West (slides) / The Hare Krishna People / Holy Places of India (Part I: The North; Part II: East, Central, West and South) (slides) / ISKCON: New Cult or Ancient Culture (slides) / The Life of Sri Caitanya (slides) / Puri—The City of Lord Jagannatha (slides) / Spark of Life / The Spiritual Frontier / Vrindavana: Land of Krishna (slides) / Vrndavan: Land of Kṛṣṇa
Jones, Clifford	The Goddess Bhagavati: Art and Ritual in South India / Kamban Ramayana / Kuttiyattam: Sanskrit Drama in the Temples of Kerala / The Serpent Deities: Art and Ritual in South India / The Worship of the Deity Ayyappan: Art and Ritual in South India
Knipe, David	A Contemporary Guru: Rajnish / Death and Rebirth in Hinduism / Hindu Pilgrimage / Hinduism in South India / An Introduction: Exploring the Religions of South Asia / The Life Cycle in Hinduism: Birth, Initiation, Marriage / Living Hinduism / Sectarian Hinduism: Lord Siva and His Worship / Sectarian Hinduism: Lord Vishnu and His Worship / Sectarian Hinduism: The Goddess and Her Worship
Long Search (series)	(See: Eyre, Ronald)

Malle, Louis	Calcutta / The Indians and the Sacred / A Look at the Castes / On the Fringes of Indian Society / Things Seen in Madras
Mead, Margaret	Bali Today . . . (with Elda Hartley) / Trance and Dance in Bali (with Gregory Bateson)
New age, Films for a (series)	(See: Hartley, Elda)
Phantom India (series)	(See: Malle, Louis)
Ray, Satyajit	Apu Trilogy: Pather Panchali; Aparajito; The World of Apu / Bala / Devi / Distant Thunder / Portrait of a City / Rabindranath Tagore
Smith, H. Daniel	Hindu Devotions at Dawn / Hindu Family Celebration: 60th Birthday / Hindu Procession to the Sea / The Hindu Sacrament of Surrender / Hindu Sacrament of Childhood: The First Five Years / Hindu Temple Rites: Bathing the Image of God / How a Hindu Worships: At the Home Shrine / India—Hinduism (slides, with Charles Kennedy) / Monthly Ancestral Offerings in Hinduism / Pilgrimage to a Hindu Temple / Radha's Day: Hindu Family Life
Smith, Huston	Hinduism: Part I; Part II; Part III / India and the Infinite: The Soul of a People (with Elda Hartley) / Krishnamurti: A Dialogue . . .
Srinivasan, Doris	The Hindu Ritual Sandhya
Staal, Frits	Altar of Fire / The Four Vedas (recording)
Syracuse University (series)	(See: Smith, H. Daniel)
Toynbee, Arnold	Four Religions (Part I and Part II)
Traditional Art and Religion in South India (series)	(See: Jones, Clifford)
University of Wisconsin (series)	(See: Binford/Camerini; also, Knipe)

TOPICAL INDEX

<table>
<tr><td>Films and
Videocassettes</td><td>Slides and
Recordings (R)</td></tr>
</table>

ANCESTRAL RITES
  Death and Rebirth in Hinduism
  Hindu Pilgrimage
  An Indian Pilgrimage: Kashi
  Monthly Ancestral Offerings . . .

Death and Rebirth in Vedic India
India—Hinduism (#104-111)

ART
  Cave Temples—Hindu
  The Goddess Bhagavati . . .
  Imminent Deities
  India and the Infinite . . .
  Kaleidoscope Orissa
  Khajuraho
  Konarak
  Madhubani Painters
  Miracle of Bali . . .
  Mirror of Gesture
  Radha and Krishna . . .
  The Serpent Deities . . .
  The Sword and the Flute
  Tantra
  Temples of Belur and Halebid

F.A.T.E.—Bengali Religious Art . . .

Slides of the Ramayana
(See also several slide sets at the end of
Chapter Two: Cultural
Background for the Study of
Hinduism)

ASHRAM
  The Avatar: Concept and Example
  A Contemporary Guru: Rajnish
  Four Holy Men . . .
  Indian Holy Men: Darshan
  On the Fringes of Indian Society
  Swami Karunananda . . .
  Swami Shyam

The Sounds of Yoga Vedanta (R)

AUROBINDO
  The Avatar: Concept and Example
  On the Fringes of Indian Society

The Mother Reading The Mother (R)

AVATARA
  The Avatar: Concept and Example
  Sathya Sai Baba . . .
  Sectarian Hinduism: Lord
    Vishnu . . .
  Vrndavan: Land of Krsna

The Life of Sri Caitanya

BALI
  Bali Today . . .
  Miracle of Bali . . .
  Trance and Dance in Bali

Golden Rain (R)

BANARAS (= Kashi)
  Banaras
  Bhismallah Khan
  Ganges River

Holy Places of India

ALPHABETICAL AND AREA INDEX TO TITLES